高等院校民航服务专业系列教材

空中乘务情境英语
（第2版）

范晔　邹海鸥　主　编
彭征宇　邓丽君　易玉婷　副主编

清华大学出版社
北京

内 容 简 介

本教材为江苏省在线开放课程"空中乘务情境会话（中英双语）"的配套教材，获评江苏省优秀培育教材，并被列入国家"十三五"规划教材。

教材编写以客舱服务工作流程为主线，以空中乘务员岗位为核心，围绕"客舱服务工作情境"，设计了"Regular On-board Service"和"Special On-board Service"两个模块，共7个大情境，28个子情境。新版教材聚焦民航业新动态，体例与内容均作了相应的更新，将行业前沿的公共卫生安全新要求融入教材，增设了 Suspected Infectious Diseases 等情境，并完成了教材的数字化改革，各章首页可扫码观看本章配套的动画视频。

教材整体设计针对空乘专业学生和社会学者，着力于分类认知任务、学习典型对话、熟悉高频语句、掌握专业词汇、应用拓展知识、探究案例分析，帮助学生领会职业标准、感悟航空文化，轻松使用英语口语应对客舱服务中的各类常规工作、个性服务和突发状况，有效内化岗位工作能力，提升职业可持续发展能力。

本书封面贴有清华大学出版社防伪标签，无标签者不得销售。
版权所有，侵权必究。举报：010-62782989，beiqinquan@tup.tsinghua.edu.cn。

图书在版编目 (CIP) 数据

空中乘务情境英语 / 范晔，邹海鸥主编 . —2 版 . —北京：清华大学出版社，2022.9（2024.8重印）
高等院校民航服务专业系列教材
ISBN 978-7-302-61722-8

Ⅰ . ①空… Ⅱ . ①范… ②邹… Ⅲ . ①民用航空—乘务人员—英语—高等学校—教材 Ⅳ . ① F560.9

中国版本图书馆 CIP 数据核字 (2022) 第 155920 号

责任编辑：张　瑜
装帧设计：杨玉兰
责任校对：周剑云
责任印制：沈　露

出版发行：清华大学出版社
　　　　　网　　　址：https://www.tup.com.cn, https://www.wqxuetang.com
　　　　　地　　　址：北京清华大学学研大厦 A 座　　邮　编：100084
　　　　　社　总　机：010-83470000　　邮　购：010-62786544
　　　　　投稿与读者服务：010-62776969, c-service@tup.tsinghua.edu.cn
　　　　　质量反馈：010-62772015, zhiliang@tup.tsinghua.edu.cn
印 装 者：三河市龙大印装有限公司
经　　销：全国新华书店
开　　本：185mm×260mm　　印　张：9.5　　字　数：235 千字
版　　次：2018 年 1 月第 1 版　2022 年 9 月第 2 版　印　次：2024 年 8 月第 5 次印刷
定　　价：49.00 元

产品编号：094876-01

本书编审委员会

张曦文（原上海航空公司 客舱经理、培训中心教员）

顾晓燕（英国维珍航空公司 资深空乘教员）

汪波（武汉职业技术学院 教研室主任、专业带头人，曾先后任职于新加坡航空公司和中国东方航空公司 空乘教员）

金枝（北京中航联盟教育投资有限公司 副总经理）

其他编审：郭恩文　白　雪

2018年，国家出台了《新时代民航强国建设行动纲要》，标志着中国正在从民航大国向民航强国转型升级，提升民航服务品质成为行业改革的重中之重，这也必然对民航从业人员，尤其是空乘服务人员的双语会话能力提出了新的要求。

编写组长期与多家航空公司保持密切合作，教材设计对接《民航乘务员岗位初级职业标准》，注重职业资格标准的规范性，兼顾了中国民用航空客舱乘务员训练合格证、空中乘务专业 1+X 等职业资格证书的英语考核要求，以期实现"无障碍"口语交流的教学目标。教材配套课程已在中国大学慕课和智慧职教等平台同步上线。

特别感谢国航、东航、南航、海航、深航、厦航、英国维珍航空等多位企业专家及多名外教的指导。这本语言能力与职业能力同步导向教材的编写离不开他们的倾情相助。

由于编者水平有限，书中难免有不足之处，恳请各位专家、教师和同学批评指正。

编　者

Regular On-board Service

SCENE 01 Boarding Service

Situation 01 Greetings and Seating Directions / 002
Situation 02 Seating / 007
Situation 03 Assisting with Overhead Storage / 012
Situation 04 Lost and Found / 017

SCENE 02 Prior to Takeoff

Situation 05 Welcome Announcement and Safety Check Announcement / 023
Situation 06 Safety Demonstrating / 028
Situation 07 Electronic Devices / 033
Situation 08 Final Safety Check / 038

SCENE 03 Cruising

Situation 09 Greetings and Airline Introduction / 042
Situation 10 On-board Entertainment / 047
Situation 11 Beverage Service / 052
Situation 12 Meals / 057
Situation 13 Duty-Free Sales / 062

SCENE 04 Landing

Situation 14 Landing Announcement, Farewell and Greeting / 067
Situation 15 Transit / Connecting and Stopover Announcement / 072

Special On-board Service

SCENE 05   Passengers with Special Needs

Situation 16   Expectant Passengers   / 080
Situation 17   Passengers with Infants   / 085
Situation 18   Unaccompanied Minor   / 089
Situation 19   Disabled Passengers   / 093
Situation 20   Senior Passengers   / 097
Situation 21   Sickness   / 101

SCENE 06   First Class Service

Situation 22   Prior to Takeoff   / 106
Situation 23   Cruising   / 111
Situation 24   Prior to Landing   / 119

SCENE 07   Dealing with Different Situations

Situation 25   Delay   / 123
Situation 26   Complaints   / 128
Situation 27   Emergency   / 133
Situation 28   Suspected Infectious Diseases   / 139

Boarding Service — Scene 01

Situation 01 Greetings and Seating Directions

任务单

主题：乘务员根据所在号位的分配站位迎宾，指引旅客入座。请根据主题和必选项、可选项的要求，编写一段英文对话。

必选项
1. 欢迎登机
2. 询问旅客的座位或请旅客出示登机牌

可选项
1. 头等舱旅客 / 商务舱旅客 / 经济舱旅客
2. 指引方向 / 引领入座
3. 问候中涉及的时间（上午 / 中午 / 下午 / 傍晚 / 晚上）
4. 欢迎客人乘坐国航 / 东航 / 南航 / 海航的航班

典型对话

经济舱乘务员指引旅客入座

FA: Good morning, Sir. Welcome aboard!
先生早上好，欢迎登机！

P: Good morning!
早上好！

FA: May I have a look at your boarding pass, please?
我可以看一下您的登机牌吗？

P: OK. I think I am on 16D.
好的，我想我的座位是16D。

FA: Your seat is in the middle of the cabin. The number is shown along the edge of the overhead compartment. Please take this aisle to the sixteenth row.

您的座位在客舱的中部，座位号标识在头顶上方的行李架边缘，请沿着过道向前至第16排。

P: Thank you!

谢谢！

FA: You are welcome.

不客气。

头等舱乘务员引导常旅客入座

FA: Good afternoon, Mr White. Nice to see you again. How are you today?

下午好，怀特先生。很高兴再次见到您。您今天好吗？

P: Fine. Thanks!

挺好，谢谢！

FA: May I have a look at your boarding pass, please?

我可以看一下您的登机牌吗？

P: Of course! Here you are.

当然可以，这是我的登机牌。

FA: Your seat number is 3A. I'll show your seat.

您的座位号是3A，请随我来。

P: OK.

好的。

FA: This way, please.

这边请。

FA: Mr White, my name is Helen. I am the cabin manager. If there is anything I can do for you, please don't hesitate to call me.

怀特先生，我是本次航班的乘务长海伦。如果您有任何需要，请随时叫我。

P: Thank you very much!

非常感谢！

高频语句

01 Welcome aboard!

欢迎登机！

02 Welcome to the flight!

欢迎乘坐本次航班！

相关表达　Welcome to Air China / China Eastern Airlines / China Southern Airlines / Hainan Airlines.

③ Good morning, Sir. Your boarding pass, please?

早上好，先生。请出示一下您的登机牌。

相关表达　Good morning, Sir. May I have a look at your boarding card, please?

④ Your seat number is 18C. Please take this aisle to the eighteenth row.

您的座位号是 18C，请沿着过道向前至第 18 排。

相关表达　Your seat is 18C. It's an aisle seat on the left. Go ahead to the eighteenth row.

⑤ The number is shown along the edge of the overhead compartment.

座位号标识在头顶上方的行李架边缘。

⑥ Your seat is in the front/middle/rear of the cabin.

您的座位在客舱的前部 / 中部 / 后部。

⑦ Let me show the way to your seat.

请随我到您的座位。

相关表达　Shall I take you to your seat?

This way, please.

专业词汇

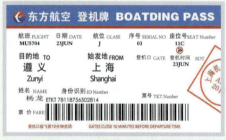

boarding pass / boarding card　登机牌

flight attendant　空姐，空少，空中乘务员

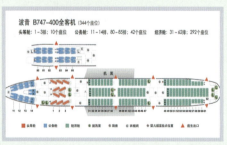

seat assignment / seat number　座位号

overhead compartment / overhead bin
飞机行李架，置物柜

拓展知识

Boarding pass, the boarding voucher for passengers to take the flight, mostly adopts the single form in Chinese and English, which is internationally accepted. At present, airlines have also introduced MMS, two-dimensional codes and other electronic boarding passes.

Boarding pass usually includes passenger's name, flight code, boarding and departure time, boarding gate, cabin (FCY), seat number and other information. F stands for first class, C stands for business class and Y stands for economy class.

The combination of numbers and letters like 15C on the boarding pass represents the passenger's seat number. A, B, C and other letters represent the number of seat columns, and numbers, such as 1, 2, 11, and 12, represent seat rows. It may appear slightly different in terms of narrow-bodied aircrafts and wide-bodied aircrafts, but essentially follows the same rules.

登机牌（boarding pass）是旅客乘坐航班的登机凭证。登机牌大多采用国际通用的中、英文单式。目前各航空公司也纷纷推出彩信、二维码等多种电子登机牌。

登机牌通常包括旅客姓名、航班代码、登机和起飞时间、登机口、舱位（FCY）、座位号等信息。F代表头等舱，C代表商务舱，Y代表经济舱。

登机牌上类似于15C的数字和字母组合代表旅客的座位号。A、B、C等字母代表座位列数，1、2、11、12等数字表示排数。不同机型的客机的座位号表示略有不同，但表示方法基本相同。

First Class　头等舱

Business Class　商务舱

Economy Class　经济舱

Dinner for First Class　头等舱正餐

> **答疑解惑**

随着科技的发展，各航空公司陆续在官网上提供"网上值机"（online seat selection）的选位服务，方便旅客在线选择自己喜爱的座位。

对于飞机座位，有人喜欢靠窗，有人喜欢靠过道，个人的情况、喜好、旅行习惯不同，对座位的要求也不一样。

问题 对于以下人群，如何有效选位？

1. 孕妇/老人/小孩
2. 尿频的人
3. 腿脚利索的年轻人
4. 晕机的人

参考答案

孕妇/老人/小孩
靠窗或中间的座位
优点：可观赏风景，安全

（过道座位位于出入口，人流量大，当旅客进出时，老人、小孩、孕妇起身让座会非常不方便。飞机上的服务，无论是发餐饮还是购物，在小孩头上进行，都是不安全的。）

尿频的人
靠过道、离洗手间近的座位
优点：进出方便，空间大

腿脚利索的年轻人
靠紧急出口的座位
优点：空间大，方便紧急撤离

晕机的人
距发动机较远又靠近窗的座位
优点：颠簸较小，噪音小

Situation 02 Seating

任务单

主题：旅客确认座位或请求调换座位。请根据主题和必选项、可选项的要求，编写一段英文对话。

必选项	1. 旅客向乘务员寻求帮助 2. 乘务员了解旅客需求，提供帮助
可选项	1. 确认座位 / 调换座位 2. 确认座位的原因，如：不确定座位在哪里 / 座位已被占 3. 调换座位的原因，如：和朋友邻坐 / 靠窗 / 靠过道 / 晕机 / 随行有婴儿 4. 乘务员及时协调解决 / 乘务员一时无法解决

典型对话

旅客确认座位

P1：Excuse me. Could you help me with my seat?
　　打扰了，您能帮我确认一下我的座位吗？

FA：Yes. Your boarding pass, please?
　　好的，我可以看一下您的登机牌吗？

P1：Here it is. My seat is 11B. But someone is sitting there.
　　给您，我的座位是11B，但是已经有人坐在那儿了。

FA：All right. Follow me, please.
　　好的，请跟我来。

(Both go ahead towards seat 11B)

(引领旅客前往 11B)

FA：Excuse me, Sir. May I see your boarding pass, please?
　　不好意思，先生，我能看一下您的登机牌吗？

P2：A second. Here you are.
　　稍等，这是我的登机牌。

FA：I'm afraid you may have taken a wrong seat. This is 11B, but your seat number is 17B.
　　先生，恐怕您坐错位置了，这里是11B，而您的座位号是17B。

P2: Oh, I got it wrong. I'm sorry!
哦，我弄错了，抱歉！

FA: It is all right.
没关系。

P1: Thank you very much!
非常感谢！

FA: My pleasure.
乐意为您效劳。

乘务员确认座位（紧急出口旁的座位）

FA: Excuse me, Sir.
打扰了，先生。

P: Yes?
什么事？

FA: You sit at the emergency exit row. Would you be willing to assist in case of any emergency?
您现在所坐的是紧急出口的位置。有紧急情况发生的时候，需要您的帮助，请问您愿意配合吗？

P: What should I do then?
那需要我做些什么呢？

FA: In normal situation, please do not touch this red handle. In emergency, could you please help us open this door and help other passengers evacuate? Please read this safety instruction card carefully.
在正常情况下，请不要触碰红色手柄。当飞机遇到紧急情况时，请您协助机组人员打开这扇舱门，帮助疏散其他旅客。这是安全须知卡，请您仔细阅读。

P: I'm not sure I could help. But I don't want to move either.
我不确定我能否帮忙，不过我也不想换座位。

FA: Sir, you need to agree to assist us during evacuation if you sit here.
先生，坐在紧急出口位置的旅客必须同意在紧急情况下帮助我们才行。

P: How?
怎么帮助？

FA: We need your help to open the exit door.
我们需要您帮忙打开紧急出口舱门。

P: Well, I will change the seat, I think.

呃，我想我还是换座位吧。

FA: All right.

好的。

旅客请求调换座位

FA: Excuse me, Madam. Did you call?

女士，您好！是您按呼唤铃吗？

P: Yes.

是的。

FA: What can I do for you?

有什么可以帮助您的？

P: The lady over there is my friend. I wonder if I could sit next to her.

那位女士是我的朋友，我们可以坐在一块儿吗？

FA: Well, I could ask the girl beside her whether she would mind changing the seat.

呃，我可以帮您询问一下她身边的女孩儿是否愿意调换座位。

P: Thank you very much!

非常感谢！

FA: But the aircraft is about to take off. May I talk with the girl after it gets into level flight?

飞机很快就要起飞了，等飞机进入平飞状态后，我再询问她，可以吗？

P: Sure. Thanks!

好的，谢谢！

高频语句

01 Excuse me, Madam. I need your help.
打扰了，女士。我需要您的帮助。

相关表达　Excuse me. Could you help me with my seat?

02 May I see your boarding pass, please?
我可以看一下您的登机牌吗？

相关表达　Could I have a look at your boarding card, please?

03 I'm afraid you are (sitting) in the wrong seat.
恐怕您坐错座位了。

④ I wonder if I could change my seat.

我可以换到其他座位吗?

相关表达　Could I switch to another seat?

May I move towards the front of the aircraft?

⑤ You may switch to another vacant seat once everyone is On-board and seated.

等旅客全部登机就座后,您可以换到其他空座位。

相关表达　Follow me. I will find an unoccupied seat for you.

I will see if there is any vacant seat.

⑥ The man over there would like to sit with his friend next to you.

那边座位的男士想和坐在您旁边的他的朋友坐一起。

相关表达　The man over there wonders whether it is all right to sit with his friend beside you.

⑦ Would you be kind enough to change to another seat?

请问您能换个座位吗?

相关表达　Would it be possible to switch the seat?

专业词汇

online seat selection　网上选座

emergency exit row / exit seat　紧急出口旁的座位

front row seat / middle seat / back seat　前排座位 / 中间座位 / 后排座位

vacant seat / window seat / aisle seat　空座位 / 靠窗座位 / 靠过道座位

拓展知识

According to Regulations on the Administration of Civil Aviation Flight Standards, if the aircraft passenger doesn't follow the instructions of the aircraft crew, either arbitrarily switching the seat, or refusing to change the seat when it is not suitable for seating near the emergency exit row, the passenger shall face a fine of up to 10 thousand *yuan*.

根据《民用航空飞行标准管理条例》，机上旅客如不听从机组成员的指挥，擅自调换座位，或者在条件不适宜时入座应急出口附近位置，且拒绝机组成员为其调换座位，将会面临最高1万元的罚款。

答疑解惑

问题 飞机没满员，空座位很多，换个位子似乎更舒服。那么，旅客可以随意调换座位吗？会引发机毁人亡的危险吗？

参考答案

旅客私自换座位，真的能影响到飞行安全吗？航空公司的工作人员表示，这绝不是危言耸听。

每次起飞前重心数据都要告知机组

飞机在起飞时，除了搭载旅客，还要搭载行李和货物。因为很多时候旅客坐不满客舱，每次搭载行李和货物的重量也不一样，所以每架飞机起飞前都要计算出重心数据，随后把数据传送给机组，机组再将数据输入到飞行计算机，来决定飞机起飞时水平尾翼的姿态，以保障飞机安全飞行。

起降走动、私自换座都会影响飞行安全

每一个旅客换完登机牌后，其座位就固定下来。旅客座位的位置决定了重心数据，如果旅客私自改变座位，而机组重心数据又没有更改，就可能对飞机飞行安全造成影响。在飞机起飞或降落时随意走动，也会危害飞行安全。

机上4个人有变动就要重新算数据

飞机自重比较大，在空中飞行时，个别的位置变动一般不会影响飞机安全，但如果座位变化较大，就会让飞机的重心改变，从而影响飞行安全。

数据传输结束后，如果有300千克的重量发生了变动（也就是约4个人的变化），就需要重新计算飞机重心数据。

以航空公司常见的空客A320系列飞机为例，满载时的起飞重量一般在70吨左右，飞机上150名旅客，假设平均体重为72千克，那么旅客的总重量也是很大的，如果配平不合理，会对飞机重心数据产生很大影响。

Situation 03 Assisting with Overhead Storage

任务单

主题：旅客摆放行李。请根据主题和必选项、可选项的要求，编写一段英文对话。

必选项
1. 旅客摆放行李时遇到困难，乘务员帮助解决困难
2. 乘务员提醒旅客行李摆放不当之处，并给予纠正
（以上两个选项任选其一作为必选项）

可选项
1. 寻求帮助：旅客不清楚行李摆放在何处/行李偏重/行李体积偏大/置物柜满了/行李超重需要托运
2. 行李摆放不当：摆放在过道/紧急出口处/行李过多占用置物柜空间/易滑落的物品放在置物柜内
3. 行李：行李箱/手拎包/笔记本/婴儿车/盒装物品/衣物等

典型对话

旅客寻求帮助

P: Excuse me.
打扰了。

FA: Yes? What can I do for you?
有什么可以帮助您的？

P: The overhead compartment is full. I'm unable to put my bag in it.
上面的行李架已经满了，我的包无处可放。

FA: Could you place it under the seat?
要不把它放在座椅下方？

P: I tried but it doesn't fit.
我试过了，但是放不进去。

FA: All right. Follow me. There may be some room in the front cabin.
好的，请跟我来，前排的客舱可能仍有些空间，可以放置。

P: Thank you!
谢谢！

FA: My pleasure.
不客气。

乘务员协助摆放行李

FA: Excuse me. Whose bag is it?

打扰一下，请问这是谁的包？

P: Mine. What's up?

我的，怎么了？

FA: Well, this lady wants to put her bag into the compartment too. But there is not enough room left. Could I lean your bag a bit to put her bag in?

这位女士想将她的包放在行李架上，但是空间有点小，能否将您的包稍微倾斜一下，把她的包放到里面去？

P: Sure. No problem.

可以，没问题。

FA: Thanks!

谢谢！

乘务员提醒行李摆放不当

FA: Whose handcart is this?

请问这是谁的手推车？

P: Mine. What's wrong?

我的，怎么了？

FA: It might fall down in case of turbulence and hurt someone. Would you please put it somewhere else?

如果发生颠簸，手推车有可能掉落砸伤旅客。能否请您将它放到其他地方？

P: Could I leave it on the aisle?

我可以把它放在过道里吗？

FA: I'm afraid not. Would you mind if I take care of it? I'll put it in the cloakroom and bring it to you before landing. Is that OK?

恐怕不行。您如果不介意的话，我将它放在衣帽间里，下飞机前再给您拿过来，可以吗？

P: All right. Thanks quite a lot.

好的，太感谢了。

FA: You are welcome.

乐意效劳。

高频语句

01 Could you help me with my luggage?
请问能帮忙放下行李吗?
相关表达　Could you do me a favor?

02 Excuse me. Whose bag is it?
打扰了,请问这是谁的包?
相关表达　Excuse me. Whose handcart is this?

03 What's up?
怎么了?
相关表达　What's wrong?

04 Would you like me to put your bag somewhere else?
我可以将您的包放到别处吗?
相关表达　Would you mind putting your bag over there?

05 I'm afraid you can't leave your bag on the aisle.
抱歉,过道上不能放行李。
相关表达　I'm sorry, but baggage couldn't be left on the aisle.

06 The overhead compartment is full.
置物柜已满。
相关表达　There's no room left in the overhead compartment.

07 In case of turbulence, the suitcase might fall and hurt someone.
遇到气流颠簸,行李箱可能会滑落,伤到他人。

专业词汇

baggage / luggage　行李
registered baggage / oversized baggage　托运的行李 / 超规的行李
lost baggage / damaged baggage　丢失的行李 / 损坏的行李
delayed baggage / misdirected baggage　延误的行李 / 运错地址的行李

拓展知识

　　Since January 1st, 2017, Regulations on the Regular Management of Flights and Regulations on China Civil Aviation Security Screening have been officially implemented. The new regulations have come into force. What are the new regulations on luggage?

1. What's the baggage allowance? What items can a passenger take with him / her?

Carry-on baggage: The allowance is 5 kg and the maximum size is 55cm*40cm*20cm.

Free baggage allowance: Most of the airlines have the allowance of 40 kg for first-class passengers, 30 kg for the business class, and 20 kg for the economy class. The maximum volume is 100cm*60cm*40cm.

Carry-on items:

Small and valuable items, such as cash and credit cards;

Emergency items, such as drugs and passport;

Items that cannot be replaced, such as the diploma;

Fragile items, such as glasses, mobile phones, cameras and lenses.

2. What to keep in mind if I bring items such as mobile phone, portable battery or cosmetics with me On-board?

If you want to take a portable battery along, follow these three rules. First, every passenger shall not take along more than two portable batteries. Second, its capacity cannot exceed 160 Wh. If the capacity is less than 100 Wh, you can directly take it on the plane. If the capacity is between 100 Wh and 160 Wh, you should take it on the plane only after the approval of the airline. Third, the portable battery should have a clear brand. It is not allowed to take the portable battery with unclear identification, three Nos (no produce date, no certification and no manufacturer), poor quality and uncertain capacity.

Samsung NOTE7 mobile phones are prohibited to be brought on the aircraft, charged and checked.

Carry-on cosmetics cannot exceed 100 mL, and it can be checked once it exceeds 100 mL.

从2017年1月1日起,《航班正常管理规定》《民用航空安全检查规则》正式实施,乘坐飞机开始执行新的规定了,关于行李有哪些新规呢?

1. 行李限重是多少,哪些物品可以随身携带?

对于随身行李,限重5千克,最大体积55cm*40cm*20cm。

对于免费托运的行李,大多数航空公司规定为:头等舱限重40千克,公务舱限重30千克,经济舱限重20千克,体积最大100cm*60cm*40cm。

随身携带的行李为:

小而贵重的物品,如现金、信用卡等;

急用物品,如药品、护照等;

不可取代的物品,如毕业证等;

易碎品,如眼镜、手机、相机、镜头等。

2. 手机、充电宝、化妆品等常用物品怎么带，哪些不能上飞机？

携带充电宝必须遵循这三点：①每位旅客携带的充电宝个数不能超过两个；②容量不能超过 160Wh，容量小于 100Wh 的可直接带上飞机，容量为 100Wh ~ 160Wh 的需经航空公司同意才可带上飞机；③需要有明确的商标品牌，标识不清、"三无"产品、质量不过关、不能确定容量的充电宝都不允许携带。

三星 NOTE7 系列手机禁止带上飞机、充电及托运。

随身携带的化妆品不能超过 100 毫升，超过 100 毫升的需要托运。

答疑解惑

有些旅客可能不太清楚随身能带多大的行李，或者未能听从值机和安检人员的告知，带着重量和尺寸超标的行李登机，结果登机后，因为种种原因需要补办托运手续。而这个时候往往临近航班起飞时间，很容易造成旅客来不及办理行李托运手续而误机，或者行李不能随机抵达，给旅行带来不便。

问题 机舱那么大，而且明明舱内地板可以放下，为什么不让带超标行李上飞机呢？

参考答案

原因一：当飞机起飞时，机长是根据地面报告的旅客重量、行李重量、货邮重量以及加注的燃油重量来计算飞机总重量的，而客舱里行李超重部分并没有被纳入计算中。于是，"三超"行李越多，计算偏差越大，势必会影响机长对飞机总重量的判断，从而影响对飞机起飞速度的设定。一旦飞机总重量超过飞机起飞的允许重量，飞机就不能顺利拉起，甚至造成飞行事故。

原因二：由于飞机客舱行李架空间和承重能力有限，当飞机遇到颠簸或在其他特殊情况下，飞机所产生的巨大冲撞力可能会使行李架的箱门打开，行李被甩出，这种情况的后果可想而知。一旦发生紧急情况需要撤离，这些物品就随时都会变成"拦路虎""绊脚石"，甚至是砸伤旅客的凶器。

原因三：在空难发生时，行李架上的行李会坠落到过道上影响逃生，甚至造成人身伤害，给救援带来障碍和困难。因此，机长有权要求旅客随身携带的行李不得超过规定。如果发现旅客违规，可以告知其办理托运；如旅客拒绝，可劝其离开飞机，还可要求地面的警察予以协助。旅客在登机后，机组人员也有权对旅客的行李进行检查。

因此，旅客在出行前，应了解乘机须知，掌握托运行李、可携带行李及违禁物品的相关规定，提前对自己的行李进行分类整理。乘坐飞机时，一定要按规定携带行李，严禁携带"三超"行李登机，否则机场安检人员、登机口验票人员、乘务人员随时可能要求旅客返回值机柜台进行行李补运。这样旅客将耗费更多时间折回托运，很多时间本身就不充裕的旅客更是因此错过航班，给自己带来麻烦。

Situation 04 Lost and Found

任务单

主题：旅客行李或物品丢失，乘务员给予帮助。请根据主题和必选项、可选项的要求，编写一段英文对话。

必选项
1. 旅客发现行李不见了，向乘务员求助
2. 乘务员及时了解情况，给予帮助

可选项
1. 刚登机 / 就座后
2. 手提包 / 笔记本 / 背包或其他物品不见了
3. 与旅客沟通顺畅 / 旅客不易沟通
4. 旅客丢失 / 捡到物品

典型对话

旅客发现手提包不见了

P: Excuse me, Miss.
打扰了，小姐。

FA: Yes? What can I do for you?
有什么可以帮助您的？

P: I seem to have lost my handbag at the airport. Could you help me?
我的手提包好像在机场弄丢了，您能帮助我吗？

FA: I'm sorry to hear that. We'll try our best to help you.
听到这个消息我很难过，我们会尽力帮助您的。

P: Thanks!
谢谢！

FA: Please give me your name, phone number, address, and a detailed description of your handbag.
请告诉我您的姓名、电话号码、地址，并请详尽描述一下您的手提包。

P: All right. Here it is. When will I get my handbag?
好的，我来写给您。我什么时候可以拿回我的手提包？

FA: It is hard to say. We'll now contact our ground staff to look for it.
这很难说，我们现在就联系地服人员帮您寻找。

P： There are some important documents in the bag. Please!

包里有重要的文件，所以拜托啦！

FA： I see. As soon as we find it, we'll contact you immediately.

我理解您的心情，一旦找到，我们会立刻联系您。

P： Thank you very much!

非常感谢！

旅客捡到贵重物品

P1： Excuse me, Miss.

打扰了，女士。

FA： Morning, Sir. Can I help you?

早上好，先生。有什么可以帮助您的?

P1： I just found a wallet at the corner. Maybe someone lost it.

我刚刚在角落里发现了这个钱包，估计是有人不小心弄丢了。

FA： Oh, thanks a lot. I'll deal with it.

啊，太感谢您了，我来处理。

P1： You are welcome.

不用谢。

FA： Morning, ladies and gentlemen. Anyone who lost a wallet please contact our flight attendants to get it back.

各位旅客，早上好。如果有人丢失了钱包，请与空乘人员联系。

P2： Hello. I heard the announcement. I just can't find my wallet.

您好！我刚刚听到广播，我的钱包不见了。

FA： All right. Come with me, please.

好的，请跟我来。

(Both go towards the front of the cabin)

(引领旅客前往机舱前部)

FA： Would you please tell me how the wallet looks like and what is in it?

您可以描述一下您钱包的样子以及里面有什么东西吗?

P2： It is blue. There are two tickets, a photo of my family, a little cash and some credit cards.

它是蓝色的，里面有两张车票、一张我的全家福照片、少量的现金和一些信用卡。

FA： All right. Here you are. Take care!

好的，给您，请妥善保管。

P2： Thanks quite a lot!

非常感谢！

高频语句

01 I seem to have lost my bag.
我的包不见了。
相关表达　I can't find my bag.

02 I am sorry to hear that.
真遗憾。

03 When and where did you lose it?
您在什么时间、在哪儿遗失它的?

04 Please give me your name, address, phone number and a description of your lost baggage.
请告诉我您的姓名、地址、电话号码，并请您描述一下您遗失的行李。
相关表达　Would you please tell me your name, address, phone number and everything about your missing luggage?

05 Our ground staff will contact you as soon as they find it.
我们的地勤人员找到后会即刻联系您。
相关表达　If it is found, we'll contact you immediately.
　　　　　Once our ground staff find it, they will get contact with you.

06 You need to complete an irregularity report form.
请您填写一张行李异常报告表。
相关表达　You need to fill out an irregularity report form.

专业词汇

lost and found　失物招领
ground staff　地勤人员

irregularity report form　行李情况异常表
delayed baggage report　行李延误报告单

拓展知识

How to find lost check-in baggage?

1. Immediately go to the baggage counter of the airline that you take

Usually, the staff at the baggage counter will simply ask about the appearance of the baggage, such as size, style, and color and name tag.

There is no need to worry about the language barrier at overseas airports. Usually, the baggage counter is equipped with the common baggage templates in a variety of styles, colors and sizes so as to choose the closest style.

Then, the staff will check the baggage's whereabouts according to the receipt of the checked baggage, which is the small ticket affixed to the back of the boarding pass, through the "World Tracer".

If you fail to find the baggage's whereabouts in the "World Tracer", you may search for it through the appearance of the baggage, for your baggage may be lost on the way from the airplane to the arrival hall, or the baggage missed the scanning of the baggage check.

2. Receive the registration number of delayed baggage

When you inquire into the baggage, you will receive a "Registration Number of Delayed Baggage". With this number, you can check the current baggage status on the airline's website and modify the baggage's delivery information and contact information when necessary.

3. Find the right place to wait

If the baggage has been identified and will arrive at the airport within a few hours, it is recommended to wait at the airport, because the airport will arrange the time and the route to deliver the delayed baggage.

If you cannot determine the whereabouts of baggage, or determine the whereabouts of the luggage, but it cannot be served on the same day, you can leave a delivery address and contact information, and then leave the airport.

In either case, make sure you get "the Registration Number of Delayed Baggage" and then leave the airport.

4. Obtain compensation

According to different procedures of the airlines that you take, if you have not received the lost luggage after certain time of the report for the loss, which is usually 72 hours to seven days, the baggage is most probably lost, and you need to be ready to enter the procedure of compensation.

The usual procedure for compensation begins with a form called "Missing Property Questionnaire", the main part of which is a list of the items within the lost baggage that needs to be specific to the time and price for each item in order to calculate for compensation.

如何寻找丢失的托运行李？

1. 立即前往所乘坐航空公司的行李服务柜台

通常行李服务柜台的工作人员会先简单询问行李的外观问题，比如大小、样式、颜色、是否挂了姓名牌等。

在境外机场也不用担心语言问题，通常在行李服务柜台都会准备各种常见行李箱包样式、颜色和大小的模板，以便选出最接近的外观。

然后工作人员会根据托运行李时的回执——也就是贴在登机牌背面的那张小票——通过"全球行李查询系统"来查询行李的下落。

如果在"全球行李查询系统"中暂时没能查询到行李的下落，如行李掉落在了从飞机到大厅的路上，或行李在某次扫描行李票时被遗漏等，那么可通过之前询问的行李外观寻找。

2. 领取延误行李登记编号

查询行李时，会得到一个"延误行李登记编号"。使用这个编号，可以在航空公司的官网上查询到目前的行李状态，并可在必要时修改行李递送信息和联系方式。

3. 找对等待的位置

如果已经确定了行李的下落，并且在几个小时以内就能到达所在的机场，建议就在机场等。因为机场递送延误行李是会安排时间段和线路的。

如果暂时无法确定行李下落，或者确定了行李下落但无法在当天送达，可以留下一个运送地址和联系方式，然后离开机场。

无论哪种情况，都一定要确保你拿到了"延误行李登记编号"再离开机场。

4. 获取赔偿

根据所搭乘航空公司的不同流程规定，在报失一定时间后（通常是72小时~7天），如果还没有收到丢失的行李，那么需要做好行李丢失的心理准备，进入赔偿程序。

通常的赔偿程序开始于一个叫作"丢失行李调查表"的表格。这个表格的主要内容是列出丢失行李内装物品的清单，需要具体到每件物品的购买时间和购买金额，以便赔偿时计算。

答疑解惑

旅途中，乘飞机大多需要行李托运，但有时会遭遇托运行李丢失的情况。据粗略估计，全球每两百个机场托运行李就有一件遗失。

问题 如何防患于未然，避免托运行李丢失？

参考答案

在行李上做醒目的标记并挂上行李牌
在同一个航班上，有几个相似甚至一模一样的行李箱是再正常不过的情况。可以在箱子外观上做装饰以进行区别：比如给箱子戴上箱套、贴上箱贴、挂上行李牌等。

按时 CHECK IN 并办完托运手续
在这期间，注意行李票是否妥善贴在了行李上，并向地勤人员确定行李是直挂目的地还是需要自己在中转地提取再重新托运。

在订票时注意中转时间
给自己和行李转运都留出充裕的时间。

买保险
在购买机票或旅行保险时，考虑给行李也买份保险。

及时清理过往行李票
如果箱子上贴满了行李票，行李分拣员很难确认到底哪个才是他这次应该扫描的那张，可能因此出错。

Prior to Takeoff

Scene 02

Situation 05 Welcome Announcement and Safety Check Announcement

任务单

主题：	飞机起飞前，乘务员进行客舱广播，欢迎旅客并做安全提醒。请根据主题和必选项、可选项的要求，编写一段英文广播稿。
必选项	1. 乘务员对旅客乘坐本次航班表示欢迎 2. 乘务员提醒安全事项 （以上两项任选其一）
可选项	1. 欢迎语：介绍飞行距离、时间、速度等 / 介绍航线 / 介绍客舱设备 / 提醒坐在紧急出口旁的旅客注意相关事宜 / 飞机起飞前提醒旅客注意相关事宜 2. 安全事项：行李摆放 / 安全带 / 座位及脚踏板 / 安全出口等 3. 早上 / 中午 / 下午 / 晚间 4. 国航 / 南航 / 东航 / 川航等

典型对话

乘务员向旅客表示欢迎并介绍飞行距离等信息

Good afternoon, ladies and gentlemen.

Captain Helen and her crew welcome you aboard flight CA1501 to Shanghai. The flight distance between Beijing and Shanghai is 1,160 kilometers. Flight time will be one hour and 25 minutes. We'll be flying at an altitude of 9,000 meters and at an average speed of 800 kilometers per hour. We are taxiing and will be takeoff immediately. Please remain seated and make sure that your seat belt is securely fastened. Wish you have a pleasant journey!

女士们、先生们，下午好！

欢迎您乘坐 CA1501 次航班前往上海。由北京到上海的空中飞行距离为 1 160 千米。预计空中飞行时间是 1 小时 25 分钟，巡航高度为 9 000 米，飞行速度平均每小时 800 千米。飞机正在滑行，很快就要起飞。请您在座位上坐好，系好安全带。祝您旅途愉快！

乘务员客舱安全检查广播

Good afternoon, ladies and gentlemen.

The crew member of Air China have the pleasure to welcome you aboard. In preparation for departure, please be seated, fasten your seat belt. Make sure your seat back is upright, and your tray table is stowed. We also ask you to open the window shade. This is a non-smoking flight. Smoking is not permitted in the cabin or lavatories. Tampering with or destroying the lavatory smoke detector is prohibited. Hope you have a pleasant flight!

女士们、先生们，下午好！

欢迎您乘坐中国国际航空公司的航班。飞机很快就要起飞了。现在乘务员将进行安全检查。为了您的安全，请您在座位上坐好、系好安全带、调直座椅靠背、收起小桌板、打开遮光板。本次航班为禁烟航班，在客舱和盥洗室内严禁吸烟。严禁擅自改动或损坏盥洗室的烟雾探测器。祝您旅途愉快！

旅客询问航班相关信息

（Singapore Airlines, Flight SQ827）

（新加坡航空，SQ827 次航班）

FA：Excuse me, Madam. What can I do for you?

您好，女士。有什么可以帮您的？

P：I wonder how long it will take to Singapore.

我想知道多久可以到新加坡。

FA：Usually around 5 hours and 20 minutes.

通常 5 小时 20 分钟左右。

P：What time will we arrive?

那我们什么时间能到？

FA：We are estimated to arrive at Singapore Changi Airport around 13:25.

航班预计会在 13:25 左右抵达新加坡樟宜机场。

P：Is there any time difference between two places?

两个地方有时差吗？

FA: No difference.

没有。

P: Thank you very much!

非常感谢！

FA: You are welcome.

不客气。

乘务员向旅客介绍安全事项

May I have your attention for the following safety instructions?

Your baggage should be put in the overhead compartment or under the seat.

Please securely fasten your seat belt when the seat belt sign is on.

Put your seat in the upright position for takeoff and landing.

Smoking will not be permitted during this flight.

Please locate an emergency exit nearest to you. In case of evacuation, the emergency indication lights will guide you to reach the exits.

请允许我介绍一下安全事项。请将随身行李放置在行李架上或座椅下方。当安全带信号指示灯亮起时，请务必坐好，系好安全带。飞机起飞和降落时，请调直座椅靠背。本次航班是禁烟航班。请注意距您最近的紧急出口位置，须紧急撤离时，请按照应急照明指示灯路线撤离。

高频语句

01 Ladies and gentlemen, welcome aboard China Southern Airlines Flight CZ3571.

女士们、先生们，欢迎乘坐南航 CZ3571 航班。

02 The flight distance between Beijing and Shanghai is 1,160 kilometers.

由北京至上海的飞行距离是 1 160 千米。

03 Ladies and gentlemen, attention, please!

女士们、先生们，请注意！

相关表达　Ladies and gentlemen, may I have your attention, please?

04 We will take off immediately.

我们即将起飞。

相关表达　The plane will take off soon.

05 Please fasten your seat belt, stow your tray table and make sure your seat back is straight up.

请您系好安全带，收起座椅靠背和小桌板。

相关表达　Please make sure that your seat belt is fastened, your seat is upright and your tray table is stowed.

专业词汇

seat belt　安全带

window shade　遮阳板

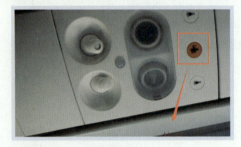

call button　呼叫按钮

reading light　阅读灯

拓展知识

What do flight attendants do after boarding in advance?

Generally speaking, the flight attendants will board the plane one hour before passengers board. First, they will check the gate and the emergency equipment in their own areas, in order to ensure that the oxygen cylinders, and other emergency supplies are available at any time. Then, they will check the cabin service equipment and cabin service facilities, including the seats, entertainment system, oven and kettle. If something is found to be out of use, they will immediately tell the maintenance personnel to repair it.

After all the equipment has been checked, the flight attendants will count and place air food and aircraft supplies. First-class flight attendants also need to prepare welcome drinks, hot towels and slippers. After all the work is done, the flight attendants will have a clearance to stop all non-operation person or non-operation items. The captain will finally release boarding instructions, and get ready to begin the flight.

乘务人员提前登机后要进行哪些工作？

一般来说，乘务人员会在旅客登机前一小时上飞机。首先，她们会根据各自负责的区域，对机门和应急设备进行查看，目的是确保飞机上的氧气瓶等应急物品处于随时可用的状态。然后查看客舱服务设备和设施，包含座椅靠背、娱乐体系、烤箱和烧水壶等，如发现有不能使用的，就立刻告诉机务人员上机进行修补。

在所有设备都查看结束以后，乘务人员就会清点和摆放航食和机上用品，头等舱的乘务人员还需要预备迎宾饮料、热毛巾和拖鞋等。在这一切作业结束后，机组会进行清舱，以杜绝一切外来人或外来物。最终，机长发布上客指令，预备开启航程。

案例分析

张女士从柬埔寨旅游回来，连呼"丢脸"，原因是同航班的几个人因为一点小事发生纠纷，在机上争执吵闹，最后被机长"请"下了飞机，航班也因此延误一小时。

问题 飞机旅客之间的口角为何会影响飞行安全？

参考答案

无论是何种机型，旅客在机上的有效活动空间都是有限的。在较为狭小的空间内，要求旅客必须有序使用过道，合理占用规定空间。如果不能有序地通行和入座，则会造成拥堵，而且可能发生碰撞，甚至引发争吵打闹。飞机在起飞、着陆和飞行过程中，都要经过严格的电脑配平，而旅客之间的争执吵闹会干扰配平，直接影响飞行安全。

Situation 06 Safety Demonstrating

任务单

主题：飞机起飞前，乘务员讲解安全须知并进行示范。请根据主题和必选项、可选项的要求，编写一段英文广播稿。

必选项	乘务员讲解安全须知
可选项	1. 救生衣的使用 2. 氧气面罩的使用 3. 安全带的使用 4. 紧急出口的位置 5. 安全须知的使用

典型对话

乘务员向旅客介绍救生衣的使用

Ladies and gentlemen, attention, please.

We are going to explain how to use the life vest to you.

The life vest is under your seat. Put the vest on, slip it over your head, fasten the buckles and pull the straps tight around your waist.

Pull the inflation tab. Please do not inflate the vest while you are in the cabin. If the vest is not inflated enough, inflate it by blowing into the mouth-pieces.

女士们、先生们，现在由客舱乘务员向您介绍救生衣的使用方法。救生衣在您座椅下方的口袋里。使用时取出，经头部穿好。将带子扣好系紧。然后打开充气阀门，但在客舱内不要充气。充气不足时，请将救生衣上部的两个充气管拉出，用嘴向里充气。

乘务员向旅客介绍氧气面罩的使用

Ladies and gentlemen, the oxygen mask is in the overhead compartment. It will drop in front of you automatically when needed. Pull the mask toward you. Place the mask over your nose and mouth and slip the elastic band over your head and breathe normally. The oxygen flow will begin within a few seconds.

女士们、先生们，氧气面罩储藏在您座椅上方行李架中。发生紧急情况时，面罩会自动脱落。请用力向下拉面罩,然后将面罩罩在口鼻处,再把带子套在头上进行正常呼吸。不久后氧气面罩将会生效。

高频语句

01 Now we would like to explain to you the safety instructions.

现在我们将向大家介绍安全须知。

相关表达　We are going to familiarize you with the safety instructions.

02 The oxygen mask is in the overhead compartment.

氧气面罩在您座椅上方行李架内。

相关表达　The life vest is located under your seat.

救生衣在您座椅下方。

03 The oxygen mask will drop automatically when needed.

发生紧急情况时,氧气面罩会自动脱落。

04 Pull the mask toward you. Place it over your nose and mouth and slip the elastic band over your head and breathe normally.

用力向下拉下面罩,置于口鼻处,将带子套在头上并正常呼吸。

05 Please make sure that your seat belt is securely fastened during takeoff, landing, air turbulence or whenever the Fasten Seat Belt sign is on.

当飞机起飞、着陆、遇到气流颠簸以及"系好安全带"指示灯亮起时,请确保系好安全带。

06 Put the vest on, slip it over your head, fasten the buckles and pull the straps tight around your waist.

取出救生衣,经头部穿好,扣好搭扣、系紧腰带。

07 If the vest is not inflated enough, inflate it by blowing into the mouth-pieces.

充气不足时,请用嘴向充气管里充气。

08 There are emergency exits on both sides of the aircraft in addition to the main entrance doors, and all exits are clearly marked.

除通常出口外,飞机客舱左右两侧均设有紧急出口处,均清晰标有"紧急出口"的标识。

09 For further information, you will find a leaflet of safety instructions in the seat pocket in front of you.

在您前排座椅背后的口袋里有安全须知卡,请仔细阅读。

专业词汇

oxygen mask　氧气面罩

life vest　救生衣

"Fasten Seat Belt" sign　"系好安全带"指示灯

emergency exit　紧急出口

拓展知识

The emergency facilities in the aircraft cabin usually include the following items.

飞机客舱的应急设施通常包括以下设备。

portable oxygen cylinders	手提氧气瓶
health and epidemic prevention package	卫生防疫包
emergency medical kit	应急医疗箱
first-aid kit	急救箱
extinguisher	灭火器
fire blanket	灭火毯
protective breathing equipment	防烟面罩
lavatory smoke detector	盥洗室烟雾探测器
automatic fire extinguisher for lavatory	盥洗室自动灭火器
folding seats for flight attendants	乘务员折叠座椅
dustbin cover for lavatory	盥洗室垃圾箱盖板
extended safety belts	加长安全带
baby safety belts	婴儿安全带
life vests for the crew	乘务员救生衣
back-up life vests for adults and babies	成人/婴儿备份救生衣
security demonstration kit	安全演示包

escape axe	逃生斧
emergency locator transmitters	应急定位发射机
escape rope on the wings	翼上逃生绳
life raft	救生筏
flash light	应急手电筒
microphone	扩音喇叭
communication systems such as internal speech and broadcasting	内话及广播等通信系统设备
emergency evacuation facilities	应急撤离设施
emergency exit signs	应急出口标记
lighting of emergency exit signs	应急出口标志的照明
control crank of emergency exit	应急出口操纵手柄
emergency exit aisle	应急出口的通道

案例分析

据昆明机场通报,曾有两名旅客在昆明机场办理登机手续时,要求地服人员安排紧急出口座位,工作人员闻到两名旅客有很大酒味,且其中一位旅客腿部有伤。工作人员依据航空公司《运行手册》中关于办理紧急出口座位的规定,拒绝办理,旅客因此情绪激动,与工作人员发生纠纷。机场民警、安保人员及时制止并将双方当事人带到公安机关调查询问。

 飞机紧急出口座位,谁都可以坐吗?乘坐紧急出口座位有何责任?

参考答案

紧急出口的座位,主要是为了方便紧急撤离。一般来说,航空公司地服会锁住紧急出口的一排座位,不在网上、自助值机机器上公开发放。

1. 什么人不能坐紧急出口座位

按照航空公司的规定,一般紧急出口处的一排位置会安排给那些身强力壮的人,老弱病残孕幼、语言不通的外国人、醉酒者、过于肥胖者及行动不便者等特殊旅客不会被安排于此。

以下人员不能坐在紧急出口:
- 两臂或双手缺乏足够的运动能力、体力或灵活性;
- 不能握住并转动操纵手柄;
- 无能力打开紧急出口舱门;
- 不满 15 岁,无人陪伴;
- 缺乏阅读、理解及语言能力;
- 视觉不佳;
- 缺乏听觉能力;
- 缺乏口头表达能力;
- 不愿意或无能力遵守出口座位相关规定。

在紧急出口旅客入座后,航空公司空乘人员会第一时间对旅客进行评估,评估分为目视评估和口头评估两种。目视评估是根据以上限制条件,看旅客是否适合坐在这里;口头评估是为旅客介绍紧急出口座位的特殊性、应急门的打开方法,告知旅客紧急情况下的职责,正常情况下千万不要触碰机门尤其是红色把手,引导其阅读紧急出口座位旅客须知和安全须知,最后观察其是否具备良好的阅读理解能力。

如果旅客无法满足须知内所列条件,即使旅客登机后坐了这个座位,乘务员也会进行座位调换。此外,在旅客身体不适、不能有效听从乘务人员指导或沟通不畅的情况下,也会进行座位调换。

2. 乘坐紧急出口座位的责任

飞机上设置"紧急出口",是为了保障全体旅客的生命安全。坐在这个位置的旅客,在享受宽敞座位的同时,也要承担起"守护者"的责任。

在飞行和降落过程中,如果发生意外事故,在机长发出指令疏散旅客时,坐在紧急出口的旅客应协助空乘人员,打开紧急出口舱门,放置好逃生滑梯或气垫,协助其他旅客逃生。

在紧急情况下,紧急出口座位的旅客要充当乘务员的援助者,在乘务员打开应急门之后,要帮助乘务员拦住客舱涌来的旅客,直到滑梯完全充满气,以免充气不足,撤离时对旅客造成伤害。滑梯完全充气后,在陆上撤离时,一名援助者要先滑下飞机,指挥旅客往风上侧远离飞机100米以上处撤离,其余援助者站在应急门旁帮助乘务员指挥旅客脱下高跟鞋,有秩序地跳下滑梯。水上撤离时,一名援助者要先从滑梯登上救生船,指挥旅客不要在救生船内站立,均匀分布在船内,其他援助者帮助乘务员指挥旅客脱下鞋子,有秩序地登船。当然,紧急情况下空乘人员也有可能受伤,如果空乘人员受伤不能开门,这时援助者就要负责打开应急门,并在开门之前观察机外情况,如果有烟、火、障碍物、机外水位过高等任何一种情况,则这个门不能开启,要指挥旅客从最近的门撤离。等到旅客成功撤离完毕后,不要忘了将受伤的乘务员也带下飞机。

Situation 07 Electronic Devices

任务单

主题：飞机起飞前，乘务员检查电子设备。请根据主题和必选项、可选项的要求，编写一段英文对话。

必选项　乘务员检查电子设备是否关闭

可选项
1. 关闭手机
2. 起飞和降落时关闭笔记本电脑、iPad

典型对话

限制使用电子设备广播

Ladies and gentlemen, in order to ensure the normal operations of the airplane navigation and communication systems, please note that certain electronic devices can not be used on board. These devices include mobile phones and remote-controlled equipment including toys. All other electronic devices including laptop computers must not be switched on until fifteen minutes after takeoff, and must be switched off when "Fasten Seat Belt" sign comes on for landing. Thank you for your cooperation!

女士们、先生们，为防止干扰飞行通信和导航系统，请您在飞行全程中不要开启和使用以下电子设备：移动电话以及遥控装置等，如遥控玩具。其他电子设备，如手提电脑等，请在飞机起飞15分钟后使用，但必须在飞机降落前、"系好安全带"指示灯亮起后关闭。谢谢您的合作！

乘务员提醒旅客关闭移动电话

FA: Excuse me, Sir. We are about to take off. Could you please switch off your cell phone?
抱歉，先生。我们的飞机马上就要起飞了，请您关闭手机。

P: I just need to make a call. It's very urgent. Just a minute. OK?
我只需要打个电话，非常重要。就一分钟，好吗？

FA: Sorry, Sir. Cell phones are strictly prohibited on the plane during taxiing and takeoff.
对不起，先生。在滑行和起飞阶段，飞机上禁用手机。

P: Please. Just a moment. It's very important.
请等一下，真的很重要。

FA: Terribly sorry, Sir. It may interfere with flight equipment. Please turn it off!
实在抱歉，先生。它有可能干扰飞行设备，请您关闭！

P: All right.
好吧。

FA: Thank you!
谢谢！

起飞前，乘务员提醒旅客关闭笔记本电脑

FA: Excuse me, Madam. The plane will take off soon. Would you please turn off your laptop?
抱歉，女士。飞机马上就要起飞，麻烦您关闭电脑。

P: Could I use it in level flight?
飞机平飞后，我可以使用吗？

FA: Yes. After the plane gets in level flight, you could turn it on.
是的，届时您可以再打开。

P: Will it be able to get access to the Internet?
那能够连上网络吗？

FA: Yes, you can get access to the Internet. We have WiFi on board.
是的，我们飞机上有 WiFi 可以连接。

P: Get it. Thanks.
明白了，谢谢。

FA: Thank you for your understanding and cooperation.
谢谢您的理解和配合。

高频语句

01 Please make sure that all electronic devices have been switched off.
请确认所有电子设备已关闭。
相关表达　Please make sure that all electronic devices have been turned off.

02 Could you please switch off your cell phone?
请您关闭手机好吗？
相关表达　Would you please turn off your mobile phone?

03 We don't want any communication devices to interfere with flight equipment.
我们不希望有任何通信仪器干扰飞行设备。
相关表达　We need to ensure the normal operations of the airplane navigation and

communication systems.

We need to make sure the airplane navigation and communication systems operate normally.

04 Cell phones are strictly prohibited on the plane during takeoff and landing.

起飞和降落阶段，机上禁止使用手机。

相关表达 Using mobile phones is not permitted during takeoff and landing.

专业词汇

navigation system   导航系统

takeoff   飞机起飞

crew member   机组成员

electronic devices   电子设备

拓展知识

In August 2016, China Civil Aviation Authority announced the revised draft of Law of the People's Republic of China on Civil Aviation, defining the following illegal interfering behaviors that may endanger the safety and order of civil aviation.

1. Hijack the aircraft in flight or on the ground.

2. Hold a hostage on an aircraft or airport.

3. Forcibly break into the aircraft, airport or aviation facilities. Rush into the cockpit of the aircraft, and intercept the aircraft forcibly.

4. Illegally bring weapons, dangerous installations, or materials to aircrafts, airports, or air traffic control units.

5. Lie about dangerous circumstances, and cause chaos. Disseminate false information

that may endanger the safety of passengers, the crew, ground personnel or the public on the aircrafts, airports or civil aviation facilities in flight or on the ground.

6. Use mobile phones or other prohibited electronic equipment on aircrafts.

7. Use kindling or smoke on aircrafts.

8. Grab seats and baggage racks. Block and grab check-in counters, security check channels and boarding gates.

9. Steal, deliberately damage or arbitrarily move the aircraft equipment, and other aviation facilities and equipment at the airport. Forcibly open the emergency hatch of the aircraft in flight.

10. Interfere or incite passengers to interfere in the execution of duty of crew or security inspector.

11. Stir up fights or cause troubles on aircrafts.

12. Break information and communication technology system for civil aviation or facilities for air-traffic control.

13. Insult or assault crew, security inspector or ground staff in the airport.

14. Other behaviors that may endanger the safety of civil aviation and order on aircrafts or airports.

In case of illegal interfering behaviors as above that endanger the safety and order of civil aviation but not severe enough for criminal penalty, or it cannot be punished in accordance with Law of the People's Republic of China on Public Security Administration Punishment, it may apply the relevant provisions of Law of the People's Republic of China on Public Security Administration Punishment for punishment. The fine could be increased to less than 50 thousand *yuan* in severe cases.

2016 年 8 月，中国民航局公布了《中华人民共和国民用航空法》修订征求意见稿，明确了下列危及民用航空安全和秩序的非法干扰行为。

1. 劫持飞行中或者地面上的航空器。

2. 在航空器上或机场扣留人质。

3. 强行闯入航空器、机场或者航空设施场所，冲闯航空器驾驶舱，强行拦截航空器。

4. 非法将武器、危险装置或者材料带入航空器、机场或者空中交通管制单位。

5. 谎报险情、制造混乱、散布诸如危害飞行中或地面上的航空器、机场或民航设施场所内的旅客、机组、地面人员或者公众安全的虚假信息。

6. 违反规定使用手机或者其他禁止使用的电子设备的。

7. 在航空器内使用火种、吸烟的。

8. 强占航空器内座位、行李架的，堵塞、强占值机柜台、安检通道及登机口的。

9. 盗窃、故意损坏、擅自移动航空器设备以及机场内其他航空设施设备，强行打开飞行中航空器应急舱门的。

10. 妨碍机组人员、安检员履行职责或者煽动旅客妨碍机组人员、安检员履行职责的。

11. 在航空器内打架斗殴、寻衅滋事的。

12. 破坏用于民用航空用途的信息和通信技术系统及用于空中交通管制设备设施的。

13. 辱骂、殴打机组人员、安检员、机场地面服务工作人员的。

14. 危及民用航空安全和扰乱航空器内、机场秩序的其他行为。

实施上述危及民用航空安全与秩序的非法干扰行为，尚不够刑事处罚的；或者依照《中华人民共和国治安管理处罚法》无法处罚的，适用《中华人民共和国治安管理处罚法》相关规定进行处罚。情节特别严重的，罚款金额可以增加到 5 万元以内。

案例分析

国内航班旅客因在飞机上玩手机而被处罚的事件已多次发生。2015 年，有旅客乘坐由长春飞往北京的航班，在飞行途中多次使用手机拨打电话，机组人员和同机旅客多次上前制止，这名旅客仍拒绝关机。飞机落地后，这名旅客被处以五日行政拘留。2015 年 8 月，在深圳前往银川的航班上，一位旅客将手机调成飞行模式继续使用并与机组人员发生激烈争吵，最后机长报警并将飞机滑回，该名旅客被处以十日行政拘留。

 玩手机会干扰飞行安全吗？航空公司在互联网服务方面是如何与时俱进的？

参考答案

玩手机会干扰飞行安全吗

中国民航局相关负责人表示，手机使用的信号频率与飞机所使用的频率同属于一个波段，有可能产生谐波干扰，影响飞行安全。民航在安全上容不得半点差错，因此，一般飞机起飞和降落阶段不允许使用手机；其他时间段是否允许使用，由各航空公司自行判断决定。

不同航空公司对于飞机上使用手机的要求各不相同。以往，国内的航空公司均表示需要全程关闭手机，现在部分航空公司允许在平飞阶段使用手机。法国航空、德国汉莎航空、美国航空表示，起飞和着陆阶段需要关闭手机，平飞阶段可以使用"飞行模式"。阿联酋航空表示，在起飞和着陆阶段必须使用"飞行模式"，平飞阶段可以正常开机。

航空事故的原因千头万绪，某一个因素造成航空事故的概率很小，很多因素重叠在一起则会发生航空事故。避免航空事故，要从各种因素上防患未然。

"空中互联"如何与时俱进

随着移动电子设备成为人们不可替代的生活必需品，航空公司也在探索和突破，在航班上推出互联网服务。东方航空的部分航班已经试运行"空中 WiFi"服务，但目前仍然只适用于平板电脑等设备，手机仍处于禁用状态。

Situation 08 Final Safety Check

任务单

主题：飞机起飞前，乘务员进行最后检查。请根据主题和必选项、可选项的要求，编写一段英文对话。

必选项	乘务员在客舱内进行安全检查
可选项	1. 将椅背放直 / 系紧安全带 / 将行李放于置物柜或座椅下方 2. 禁止吸烟 / 禁用手机 3. 不随意走动 / 起飞和着落不使用洗手间

典型对话

乘务员提醒旅客将椅背放直并系紧安全带

FA: Excuse me, Sir. Would you please return your seat back to the upright position?

打扰了，先生。请您调直座椅靠背。

P: Ok? But I don't know how. Could you please help me with it?

好的，但是我不知道该怎么弄，可以帮我调整一下吗？

FA: Sure. Just press the button on your armrest.

当然可以，您只要按一下扶手这边的按钮就可以。

P: Just like this?

这样吗？

FA: Yes. And please fasten your seat belt.

是的。也请您系好安全带。

P: I've slipped the belt into the buckle. Isn't it right?

我已经将安全带的连接片插入另外一端的锁口了，是这样吗？

FA: Yes. And you need to pull tight.

是的，您还需要将安全带拉紧。

P: Get it. Thank you!

明白了，谢谢！

FA: You are welcome.

不客气。

乘务员提醒旅客起飞前不能使用盥洗室

P: Excuse me, where is the lavatory?

您好,盥洗室在哪里?

FA: In the front and rear of the cabin. But it is locked now.

客舱的前部和后部都有,但是现在不允许使用盥洗室。

P: Why?

为什么?

FA: For the safety, nobody is allowed to use the lavatory before takeoff.

飞机马上就要起飞,为了旅客的安全,现在停止使用盥洗室。

P: When can I use it?

那我什么时候可以使用呢?

FA: When the plane gets into level flight and the seat belt sign turns off, you are free to go to the lavatory.

飞机进入平飞状态后,当安全带信号指示灯关闭后,您就可以使用盥洗室了。

P: I see. Thank you!

好的,谢谢!

FA: My pleasure.

很高兴为您服务。

高频语句

01) Now the cabin crew will make pre-flight safety check.

现在,客舱乘务员将进行飞行前的安全检查。

02) Excuse me, Sir. Would you please return your seat back to the upright position?

先生,您好。请将您的椅背调直好吗?

相关表达　Please make sure that your seat back is straight up.

03) Please check that your seat belt is fastened.

请确认您的安全带已系紧。

相关表达　Please make sure that your seat belt is securely fastened.

04) Please open the window shade.

请打开遮阳板。

05) Please do not block the emergency exit.

请勿堵住紧急逃生出口。

专业词汇

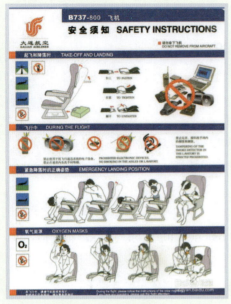

safety brochure　安全手册

emergency equipment　紧急设备

turbulence　颠簸，乱流

拓展知识

The first priority for flight attendants is safety.

Flight attendants are the forefront of airline customer service and an important bridge between passengers and airlines. Most passengers intuitively feel the intimate service from the flight attendants. However, few people realize that the first priority of flight attendants is actually to ensure safety!

Flight attendants must undergo training, and skillfully use fire extinguishers, emergency kits, defibrillators and other safety equipment, and be able to carry out basic medical assistance, such as cardiac pulmonary resuscitation (CPR). They are also required to remember the layout and emergency exits for each type of aircraft. Before becoming a flight attendant, candidates must show the ability to give first aid and other life-saving duties in a calm and professional manner. To ensure that the received training is always up-to-date, the cabin crew is retrained every year.

Before takeoff and landing, the flight attendant asks the passenger to put the seat back in its upright position, stow the tray table, open the window shade and turn off the electronic equipment, which are the necessary security procedures to ensure the safe operation of flights.

Flight attendants also receive soft skills training to deal with and mitigate the conflict or tension on the plane. They will take further action if the situation is out of control or the flight attendant is convinced that the party will pose a threat to the safety of the other passengers on the plane.

空乘人员的第一要务是安全。

空乘人员是航空公司客户服务的最前线，也是旅客与航空公司之间的重要桥梁。大多数旅客直观感受到的是空乘人员的贴心服务，但很少有人意识到空乘人员的第一要务其实是保证安全！

空乘人员必须经过训练，熟练使用灭火器、急救箱和除颤器等安全设备，能够进行基本医疗救助，如CPR心脏复苏术。他（她）们还需要记住各种飞机类型的布局和紧急出口位置。在成为空乘人员之前，候选人必须表现出能够以冷静和专业的方式处理从急救到其他救生职责的能力。为了确保接受的培训始终是最新的，空乘人员每年都会进行再培训。

在飞机起飞和降落前，空乘人员会要求旅客将座椅调回直立状态、收起小桌板、打开遮光板、关闭电子设备，这些是保证航班安全运行的必要程序。

空乘人员也会接受软技能培训，在机上发生冲突或紧张局势发展到失控状态前进行处理和缓解。如果事态已无法控制，或是空乘人员确信当事人会对机上其他旅客的安全构成威胁时，可采取进一步行动。

案例分析

2009年，英国航空公司一架飞往墨西哥的波音747在准备起飞前，空乘人员发现飞机上没有原本应该配有的烟灰缸。直到找到替代的烟灰缸后，该航班才被允许起飞，起飞时间比预定晚了至少25分钟。

 为什么飞机上严禁吸烟却必须放置烟灰缸？

参考答案

从1988年开始，美国国内航班开始明令禁止在飞机上吸烟。到了20世纪90年代末，全球大多数航空公司都开始严格执行飞机上的禁烟令，除了机舱内部的扬声器警告外，还设置有严禁吸烟的标识。

尽管如此，还是会有旅客因为控制不住自己的烟瘾而在飞机上吸烟，他们可能会因为害怕被乘务员发现而将烟头随手一丢，这样的行为可能造成不可挽回的后果，这时候就能体现在飞机上安置烟灰缸的必要性了。

虽然飞机上的烟灰缸只是起到预防作用，但是航空公司仍然对这一设置非常重视。如果飞机上的烟灰缸没有出现在它应该在的位置，这架飞机通常是不允许起飞的。

Cruising

Scene 03

Situation 09 Greetings and Airline Introduction

任务单

主题：飞机快起飞前，乘务员进行客舱广播，欢迎旅客并简要介绍航班相关信息。请根据主题和必选项、可选项的要求，编写一段英文广播稿或对话。

必选项
1. 乘务员对旅客乘坐本次航班表示欢迎
2. 乘务员介绍航班信息

可选项
1. 客舱广播 / 对话
2. 介绍航线 / 客舱设备 / 机上服务
3. 早上 / 中午 / 下午 / 晚间
4. 国航 / 南航 / 东航 / 川航
5. 航班号不限

典型对话

乘务组介绍广播

Ladies and gentlemen, this is your purser Helen speaking. Let me introduce my cabin crew to you. This is Sam, this is Eva, this is Jessica, this is Megan, and this is Taylor. We'll try our best to provide you good service and wish you a good trip. Thank you!

女士们、先生们，我是本次航班的乘务长海伦，请允许我为您介绍一下今天为您服务的乘务组成员：乘务员山姆、乘务员伊娃、乘务员杰西卡、乘务员梅根和乘务员泰勒。我们将竭诚给您带来温馨舒适的服务并祝您旅途愉快。谢谢！

航线介绍广播

Ladies and gentlemen, our plane has left Beijing for Shanghai. On this air route, we will be passing over the provinces of Hebei, Shandong and Jiangsu. And we'll cross the Yellow River, the Yangtze River, the Grand Canal and the Taishan Mountain.

女士们、先生们,我们的飞机已经离开北京前往上海。在这条航线上,我们将飞越的省份有:河北、山东、江苏,飞越的河流有:黄河、长江、大运河,飞越的山脉有:泰山。

客舱设备及服务介绍

The plane you are taking is Boeing 737-800. It can carry 169 passengers. The reading lights, air vents and call buttons are above your head. Lavatories are located in the front and the rear parts of the cabin. When the seat belt sign turns on, the lavatory can not be used.

Please do not smoke in the lavatories and cabin. We will be serving refreshments and beverages on this route.

For flight safety, do not open the baggage compartment above your head during turbulence, taxiing, takeoff, descending and landing.

We hope you will enjoy the flight! Thank you.

您现在乘坐的是波音737-800型客机。它能够容纳169名旅客。在您座位上方备有阅读灯、空调口和呼叫铃。洗手间位于客舱的前部和后部。当"系好安全带"指示灯亮起时,洗手间停止使用。

本航班为禁烟航班。这段旅途中,我们为您准备了餐点及饮料。

为确保旅途安全,请您在飞机颠簸、滑行、起飞和降落期间不要开启行李架。

祝您旅途愉快!谢谢。

旅客询问客舱设备

P: Excuse me, Miss.

打扰了,女士。

FA: Yes? What can I do for you?

有什么可以帮助您的?

P: Could you show me how to adjust the seat?

您可以告诉我如何调节椅背吗?

FA: Sure. Just press the button on the armrest of your chair.

当然可以,您按一下扶手这边的按钮就行。

P: Thank you! And I want to read for a while but it's a bit dim. Where's the light?

谢谢!我想阅读一会儿,光线有点昏暗,灯在哪儿?

FA: Here is the reading light. You could turn it on.

这是阅读灯,您可以打开它。

P： Thanks. One more question, what's this button for?

　　谢谢！还有一个问题，这个按钮有什么用途？

FA： It's "call button". Press it in case you need our help.

　　这是呼唤铃，如果您需要帮助可以按一下。

P： I see. Thanks quite a lot.

　　明白了，非常感谢。

PA： My pleasure.

　　很高兴为您服务。

高频语句

01 We'll try our best to provide you good service and wish you a good trip.

　　我们将竭诚给您带来温馨舒适的旅途。谢谢！

02 Now we are going to introduce to you the use of cabin installations.

　　下面将向您介绍客舱设备的使用方法。

　　相关表达　Now we'd like to explain to you how to use cabin facilities.

03 If you have any needs or requirements, please let us know.

　　飞行中如有任何需求，请与客舱乘务员联系。

　　相关表达　Please let us know in case of any needs or requirements.

04 Please press the call button for service.

　　如您需要服务，请按呼唤铃。

　　相关表达　If you need any help, just press the call button.

05 Just press the button on the armrest of your chair.

　　只需按一下您扶手上的按钮。

　　相关表达　Just press the button on your armrest.

专业词汇

international/domestic/arriving/departing/connecting/transit passenger　国际 / 国内 / 进港 / 出港 / 转机 / 过境旅客

captain　机长

pilot / copilot　飞行员 / 副驾驶员

chief attendant / cabin manager　乘务长

拓展知识

The plane is advanced enough to help with your jet Lay!

Recently, commercial aircraft corporations Airbus and Qatar Airways believed that their latest aircraft already had the secret of solving the jet lag, that is the Airbus A350 XWB. It has a series of design improvements to minimize the discomfort that passengers have when flying over half of the earth. The aircraft has a LED light system that automatically changes its color and simulates natural sun light and adjusts its internal procedures to adapt to human biological rhythms. The whole cabin air can be recycled by its filtering system within 2~3 minutes. It also ensures more space between seats for passengers to be more comfortable in Economy Class. More than 50% fuselage frame is made of carbon fiber reinforced plastic, which greatly reduces the weight of the aircraft. Airbus A350 XWB may go into service within 30 years in the near future.

飞机已经先进到可以帮你倒时差了！

商用飞机公司空中巴士和卡塔尔航空相信，他们的最新飞机已经拥有了解决时差综合征的秘诀，就是空客 A350 XWB。它拥有一系列设计上的改进，能将旅客飞越半个地球之后的不适感降到最低程度。机舱内的灯能够自行变换颜色，模拟自然光，内部程序也同人体的生物周期节律相适应。过滤系统每 2~3 分钟就能循环整个客舱的空气。考虑到旅客的舒适度，经济舱的座位也进行了加宽。超过 50% 的机身框架采用碳纤维强化塑料制成，大大减轻了飞机的重量。这个型号的飞机将在未来 30 年的时间内服役。

案例分析

2016 年 9 月 14 日清晨，北京首都国际机场，两名旅客因误机与值机人员发生冲突，随后撞倒值机人员，冲进登机桥，闯入机场控制区，冲到飞机前阻拦飞机出港，逼迫机组开舱门让其登机。随后，机场警方将其带走，该航班全程延误 20 分钟。

问题 为什么在飞机没有推出的情况下，不能重新打开机舱门让误机的旅客上飞机？

参考答案

根据规定，飞机关门之后没有特殊情况不能再次开舱门。点数的目的是要和舱单核对，有的旅客没有上飞机，但是托运了行李，要是没上飞机，需要把行李减下去。另外，旅客人数涉及飞机配平问题，因此只有旅客和舱单相符才能起飞。

飞机距离起飞还有20分钟（甚至半小时）就被通知不能办理乘机手续了。很多旅客以为起飞时间就是飞机离地时间。但根据民航有关规定，民航班期时刻表向旅客公布的起飞时间是指地面保障工作完毕、飞机关上客舱门和货舱门的时间，而不是飞机离地升空时间。

停止办理乘机手续到关舱门之间，机场工作人员主要要完成以下工作。

1. 将运输值机、配载人员结算的旅客人数、行李件数，结合货运装运情况，计算飞机载重，画出平衡表和重心位置，做好舱单后送交机组签字；

2. 将旅客托运的行李核对清楚后装运飞机；

3. 对办完乘机手续的旅客进行安全检查；

4. 广播通知旅客到指定登机口检票，并引导旅客登机。如登机旅客需使用摆渡车运送，那么耗时将更长；

5. 乘务员清点机上旅客人数，并与地面检票情况进行核对，防止有人漏乘。然后进行飞机起飞前的准备工作，给旅客讲解有关注意事项和机上设备使用方法，并检查行李架上的行李是否放好、旅客的安全带是否系好等。

综上所述，从停止办理乘机手续到关舱门的30分钟时间内，机场方面还需要完成大量的工作，稍有延迟就可能造成航班延误。民航已在《公共航空运输服务规则》中明确规定：100座以下飞机开始办理乘机手续的时间不迟于起飞前60分钟，100座以上飞机不迟于90分钟。为保证航班正点起飞，机场方面必须严格执行提前30分钟停止办理乘机手续的规定。

为了保证准时与安全、维护机场运营秩序，第二次开舱门放人是不可取的。关门后只有机组有权决定是否开门，但机组意见永远是统一的，不允许开门！这与是否人性化无关，飞行安全是第一位的，误机旅客只能自己承担后果与损失。

Situation 10 On-board Entertainment

任务单

主题：飞机起飞后，旅客就飞机上所提供的娱乐项目询问乘务员，乘务员及时予以解答。请根据主题和必选项、可选项的要求，编写一段英文对话。

必选项
1. 旅客询问娱乐项目
2. 乘务员给予解答

可选项
1. 询问是否提供报纸/杂志/书籍等阅读材料
2. 询问如何听音乐/观看视频等
3. 当音效/画面等出现问题时，向乘务员求助
4. 因客舱内播放视频而影响个人休息等原因，向乘务员提出诉求

典型对话

旅客询问是否有报刊可供阅读

P: Excuse me, Miss.
您好，女士。

FA: Yes?
有什么可以帮助您的？

P: Do you have any newspapers to read?
请问有报纸吗？

FA: Yes, we do. We have international newspapers like *New York Times*, *Global Times*, etc., and national newspapers, such as, *People's Daily*, *China Daily*, as well as some local newspapers, for example, *Southern Weekly*.
有的，我们有《纽约时报》、《环球时报》等国际报刊，《人民日报》《中国日报》等国内报刊，以及《南方周末》等地方报刊。

P: A copy of *Southern Weekly*, please.
请给我一份《南方周末》。

FA: Here you are. Anything else I can do for you?
好的。其他还有什么需要的吗？

P: No. Thanks!
没有了，谢谢！

FA: You are welcome.

不用谢。

旅客想听音乐

FA: Excuse me, Sir. Did you press the call button?

您好,先生,请问刚刚是您按的呼唤铃吗?

P: Yes. I'd like to listen to music but don't know how.

是的,我想听音乐,但不知道如何操作。

FA: Oh, have you got yourself a headset?

哦,您刚刚拿了耳机吗?

P: Yes. Here it is.

是的,在这儿。

FA: Just plug it into the socket.

把它插入这个插孔。

P: All right. But I can't hear it clearly.

好的,但是好像听不清楚。

FA: Well, the control buttons are on your seat armrest. You could adjust as you wish.

座椅扶手上有控键,您可随心调节音量大小。

P: OK. A second, how to change music?

好的。稍等,如何更换音乐曲目?

FA: Just press those numbers on the screen for different music.

按一下屏幕上的数字就行。

P: Oh, I see. Thank you very much!

哦,我明白了,非常感谢!

FA: My pleasure.

乐意为您效劳。

旅客因屏幕太亮寻求帮助

P: Excuse me, Miss. Could you do me a favor?

您好,女士,可以帮我一下吗?

FA: Yes. What can I do for you?

好的,有什么可以帮助您的?

P: My seat is very close to the screen. And the screen is too bright for me to sleep. Could you dim the screen?

屏幕距我太近了,而且太亮了,影响我睡觉。您可以调暗屏幕吗?

FA: I'm sorry. I can't. Would you like to wear an eyeshade? Or change the seat if possible?
很抱歉，不行呢。要不带个眼罩？或者调换座位试试？

P: Let me try the eyeshade first.
那我先戴上眼罩试试吧。

FA: A second. I will bring it over right away.
稍等，我马上给您拿过来。

P: Thanks!
谢谢！

高频语句

01 Would you like to read some newspapers or magazines?
您想翻看报纸或杂志吗？
相关表达　What would you like to read, newspapers or magazines?
　　　　　We have in-flight magazines and some newspapers. Which one would you like?

02 Hello, Sir. I saw you turn on the yellow light. What can I do for you?
您好，先生。我看您按了求助黄灯，请问能为您做什么？
相关表达　Dear Sir. Did you press the call button? Can I help you?

03 Excuse me, can you do me a favor?
您好，能帮个忙吗？
相关表达　I'd be grateful if you could help me with ...?
　　　　　Hello, could you please help me to ...?

04 We provide several kinds of music: pop music, classical music and opera.
我们提供多种类型的音乐：流行音乐、古典音乐、音乐剧。
相关表达　We have plenty of choices on the flight, ranging from pop music to opera.

05 Just press the button on your armrest.
只需按一下您扶手上的按钮。

06 You can adjust the screen brightness by pressing this button.
您可以按这个按钮来调节屏幕亮度。
相关表达　You can choose different kinds of music by pressing these buttons.
　　　　　您可以按这些按钮来调换不同的音乐。
　　　　　In case you want to adjust/change the language of the movie, just press this.
　　　　　您可以按这个按钮来调换语言。

Do you get yourself a headset?

您拿耳机了吗?

相关表达　Could I have a new pair of headsets?

请问能换一副新耳机吗?

Could you pass me your headset?

请将您的耳机给我。

There is something wrong with the headset. I will change it for you.

这个耳机坏了,我给您换一个。

专业词汇

in-flight entertainment　机上娱乐

headset　耳机

eyeshade / eye mask　眼罩

LCD monitor　液晶显示器

拓展知识

In-flight entertainment of Air China

At an altitude of 10,000 meters, Air China provides a variety of aircraft magazines and newspapers, 12 music channels and eight classic films which are elaborately selected by five experts, including John Woo, Jia Zhangke and Xie Fei, bringing a different entertainment experience to your journey.

On the deluxe wide-bodied aircraft, Air China also provides you with the advanced self-selected audio-visual entertainment system AVOD. There are dozens of domestic and foreign classic bilingual movies, hundreds of music CDs and a variety of leisure games for you, allowing you to enjoy your own entertainment trip above the clouds.

中国国航机上娱乐

万米高空，中国国际航空公司为旅客准备了多种航机杂志和报纸、12 个机上音乐频道、由包括吴宇森、贾樟柯、谢飞等著名导演在内的五位专家精心挑选的八部经典影片，给旅途带来不一样的娱乐体验。

在豪华宽体客机上，还配备了先进的自选式机上视听娱乐系统 AVOD。数十部国内外经典双语电影、数百张音乐 CD 和多款休闲游戏供旅客自由选择，让旅客在云端也能享受属于自己的娱乐之旅。

答疑解惑

由于在飞机上手机和相机都要关机或处于飞行模式，旅客在飞机上可选的娱乐方式较为单一。一直以来，飞机的舱内娱乐系统都是各航空公司吸引旅客的重要方式。

问题 请举例说明国内外航空公司提供哪些舱内娱乐方式。

参考答案

新加坡航空公司现在已推出定制娱乐服务。在登机之前，旅客可使用智能手机应用定制节目单，包括众多电影、电视节目、音乐等；登机之后，还可使用手机阅读电子书或路线图。

Situation 11　Beverage Service

任务单

主题：飞行途中，乘务员要为旅客提供饮品。请根据主题和必选项、可选项的要求，编写一段英文广播或对话。

必选项	乘务员为旅客提供饮品
可选项	1. 播放饮品服务广播 / 旅客自行提出所需的饮品 2. 提供软饮料，如可乐、雪碧、芬达等 3. 提供茶 / 咖啡 / 酒 4. 免费饮品 / 付费饮品 5. 饮用完毕，回收清理

典型对话

乘务员广播饮料服务

Ladies and gentlemen, may I have your attention, please?

We are going to provide beverage service. Tea, coffee, mineral water, orange juice, Coke and Sprite will be served. You may choose what you like. Please put down the table in front of you and straighten up your seat back for the convenience of the passenger behind you. Thank you!

女士们、先生们，现在客舱乘务员将为您提供饮料服务。有茶、咖啡、矿泉水、橙汁、可乐、雪碧等敬请选用。请您放下小桌板。为方便您后面的旅客，请您调直座椅靠背。谢谢！

旅客想喝咖啡

P: Excuse me, Miss. Could you do me a favor?
　　女士，您好。可以帮个忙吗？

FA: What can I do for you, Sir?
　　有什么可以帮助您的，先生？

P: Could you please bring me a cup of hot coffee?
　　能否给我一杯热咖啡？

FA: Sure. Black or flat white?
　　当然可以，请问是黑咖啡还是牛奶咖啡？

P: Black, please. Thank you!

黑咖啡，谢谢！

FA: All right. Here you are. Be careful. It's hot!

好的，给您，当心烫！

P: I will. Thanks!

好的，谢谢！

FA: You could call me if you want to refill the coffee.

如果您想续杯，请叫我。

P: Get it. Thank you very much!

好的，非常感谢！

旅客想喝酒

FA: Hello, Sir. Can I help you?

您好，先生。有什么可以帮您的？

P: I have a question.

我想问一下。

FA: Yes?

请讲。

P: Are all the drinks on the plane free?

机上所有的饮品都是免费的吗？

FA: All the soft drinks are free to all passengers while bar service is free to first class and business class passengers.

所有的软饮料都是免费的，部分酒水只对头等舱和商务舱旅客免费。

P: Well, what if I would like to have some wine?

好吧，那我想喝杯酒可以吗？

FA: It is also available to economy class passengers at a reasonable price.

当然，经济舱旅客支付一定费用亦可享用。

P: OK. What kinds of alcoholic drink do you offer?

有哪些种类的酒？

FA: We have red wine, white wine, whisky and brandy.

红酒、白酒、威士忌和白兰地。

P: A glass of red wine, please!

一杯红酒，谢谢！

FA: Here it is.

您的红酒。

P: Thanks!

谢谢!

高频语句

01 What would you like to drink?

您想喝什么?

相关表达　Do you need any drinks?

02 We have both cold drinks and hot drinks, such as coffee, tea, juice, coke, beer and cock tail.

我们提供冷饮和热饮,如咖啡、茶、果汁、可乐、啤酒和鸡尾酒。

相关表达　We will provide you with cold drinks, such as, mineral water, fruit juice, Sprite, Pepsi and Coca Cola. The hot drinks like hot water, coffee and tea are also available.

03 Would you like some ice with your drink?

您的饮料要加冰块吗?

相关表达　Would you like cream or sugar with your coffee?

04 How about having a cup of hot coffee?

来一杯热咖啡怎么样?

相关表达　Would you like to have a cup of hot coffee?

05 Is it OK to have another glass of juice?

还可以再来一杯果汁吗?

相关表达　Could I have one more cup of juice?

06 Here is your coffee and sugar.

这是您的咖啡和糖。

相关表达　Here you are.

专业词汇

beverage / soft drinks　饮料(统称)/ 软饮料(不含酒精的饮料)

black tea / lemon tea / green tea / jasmine tea　红茶 / 柠檬茶 / 绿茶 / 茉莉花茶

soda water / mineral water / ice water　苏打水 / 矿泉水 / 冰水

iced coffee / black coffee　冰咖啡 / 黑咖啡

拓展知识

Drinks on the aircraft

There are five kinds of basic drinks on the aircraft, including juice (apple juice and orange juice), alcohol, tea, coffee and mineral water, which are available in all types of aircrafts. Except those cheap airlines, most airlines offer unlimited service, so passengers can enjoy it as much as they like. First class and business class offer a rich range of wines. passengers can also ring the bell for flight attendants to provide drinks.

In addition, there are another three options available.

First, beer is available on the aircraft, and different airlines offer different styles of beer. The origins of the beers are mostly the countries of the airlines.

Second, three to ten kinds of cocktail are also available, which depend on cabins. The flight attendants have received professional training to mix drinks, basic types anyway.

Third, hot chocolate is also available on the plane, besides coffee and tea.

飞机上的饮品

机上的基本饮品有五种，包含果汁（苹果汁与柳橙汁）、酒类、茶、咖啡与矿泉水。各种舱型都会提供上述饮品，并且除廉价航空外，大多数航班都提供无限畅饮服务，所以旅客们可以尽情享用。头等舱和商务舱的酒水选择通常更为丰富。可以按铃请乘务员提供饮品。

除以上饮品外，还有以下三种饮品可供选择。

第一，机上会提供啤酒。不一样的航空公司提供的啤酒不尽相同，产地基本为航空公司所属国家。

第二，机上会提供三至十种调酒（依座舱的不同而定）。乘务员都经过专业调酒训练，可调制基本款式。

第三，除咖啡与茶外，热巧克力也是航班可提供的热饮品。

答疑解惑

案例：旅客酒后乘坐飞机，因对经济舱座位不满，强行更换商务舱座位，被拒绝后在机舱内吵闹，最后被拒载。

问题 在飞机上（登机时/飞行途中）遇到醉酒旅客，该如何应对？

参考答案

乌鲁木齐国际机场候机楼派出所曾处理过这样一宗闹事事件：派出所值班室接到机场现场运行指挥中心通报称，有醉酒旅客在机上闹事，请求派出所派警维持秩序。

值班室民警立即出警前往登机口，到场后在商务舱座位上发现一名浑身酒气的旅客，询问该旅客，但其不配合调查。经询问机组人员得知，该旅客在检票登机后直接坐在了商务舱的座位上，当乘务员要求其按照票面对号入座时，该旅客表达了强烈不满，并对乘务员进行语言侮辱，随后机组报告现场运行指挥中心报警。

旅客在买票时可以自行选择乘坐商务舱还是经济舱，但登机后必须按照票面对号入座，不能更换座位。经过警方与机组人员劝说后，该旅客依然不为所动，为了不影响后面登机的旅客正常出行，机长决定拒绝承运该旅客。随后民警将该旅客强制带离飞机，其三名同行者也表示放弃行程，被一同带回派出所值班室审查。

Situation 12 Meals

任务单

主题：飞机飞行途中，乘务员为旅客提供用餐服务。请根据主题和必选项、可选项的要求，编写一段英文广播或对话。

| 必选项 | 乘务员为旅客提供用餐服务 |

可选项
1. 播放饮品服务广播
2. 乘务员询问旅客用餐需求 / 旅客提出特殊用餐需求
3. 提供餐前小食
4. 提供正餐 / 快餐
5. 免费用餐 / 付费用餐
6. 用餐完毕，回收清理

典型对话

用餐服务广播

Ladies and gentlemen, we will be serving you with the meal. We have prepared chicken rice and beef noodles. Welcome to make your choice. Please put down the tray table in front of you and straighten up your seat back for the convenience of the passenger behind you. Thank you!

女士们、先生们，现在我们准备为您提供餐食服务。我们精心准备了鸡肉米饭和牛肉面条，欢迎您选用。请您放下小桌板。为方便其他旅客，请您调直座椅靠背。谢谢！

乘务员发放正餐

FA: Excuse me, Madam. Dinner is coming. Please put down the tray table.
女士，您好。为方便用餐，请放下小桌板。

P: What's for dinner?
有些什么？

FA: Chicken rice and beef noodles. Which one do you prefer?
鸡肉米饭和牛肉面条，您需要哪一种？

P: Well, chicken rice, please.
鸡肉米饭吧，谢谢！

FA: Here you are. Enjoy the meal.

您的鸡肉米饭，用餐愉快。

P: A second. May I have an extra helping when I finish this one?

对了，我吃完后可以再要一份吗？

FA: Well, I need to serve all the passengers first. It's a full flight today.

我发完所有餐食后如果有富余的一定给您，但是今天满客。

P: All right. Thank you!

好的，谢谢！

FA: You are welcome.

不客气。

旅客提出特殊用餐需求

P: Excuse me, Miss.

您好，女士。

FA: Yes? Can I help you?

有什么可以帮您的？

P: I heard the meal service announcement. I'm a vegetarian. Do you have vegetarian meal for me?

我刚刚听了用餐广播，我是素食者，有我的素食餐吗？

FA: Have you mentioned your requirement when booking the ticket?

您订购机票时，提交了特殊餐食申请吗？

P: No. I forgot. Quite sorry for that.

没有，我忘记了，真不好意思。

FA: Well, we have bread. Will it be OK?

没关系，我们有面包，可以吗？

P: All right. Thank you very much!

可以的，非常感谢！

FA: My pleasure.

乐意效劳。

高频语句

01 Could you please straighten up your seat and put down your tray table?

请将您的椅背调直并放下小桌板。

相关表达　Could you please return the seat back to the upright position and lower the tray table?

Would you please sit straight and open your tray table?

(02) What would you like for dinner? We have noodles and rice.
您想吃什么？我们提供面条和米饭。

相关表达　We have chicken over rice and bacon omelet with spaghetti. Which one would you prefer?

What do you prefer, smoked ham or fish?

(03) May I have an extra bun and salad?
我可以再要一份面包和沙拉吗？

相关表达　Is it possible for me to have an extra bun and salad?

(04) Thank you for waiting. Here you are. Anything more?
让您久等了，谢谢。这是给您的。请问还有什么需要吗？

(05) Have you mentioned your requirement when you booked the ticket?
请问您在订票时说明您的用餐要求了吗？

相关表达　Have you reminded us of the special requirement when booking the flight?

(06) You're welcome. Enjoy the meal.
不客气。祝您用餐愉快。

相关表达　My pleasure. Enjoy it.

(07) Excuse me, Sir. May I clear up your tray table now?
先生，打扰一下，现在可以清理您的小桌板了吗？

相关表达　Hello, Sir. Could I clear up the tray table now?

专业词汇

special meal (vegetarlan / gluten free / kosher / halal)　特殊饮食（素餐 / 无麸麸食品 / 犹太教食品 / 清真食品）

chicken rice / pork rice / beef noodles　鸡肉米饭 / 猪肉米饭 / 牛肉面条

buttered toast / French toast / white bread / brown bread　奶油土司 / 法国土司 / 白面包 / 黑面包

paper towel / napkin / toothpick　纸巾 / 餐巾 / 牙签

拓展知识

Gossip about aircraft catering

On the plane, not all food can be eaten. Passengers should eat fish without fishbone and meat without bones. As the aircraft often undergo turbulence during the flight, passengers will be prone to choking if they eat some hard food or fish with bones.

It's also different in the variety of the food on the same flight, in terms of First Class and Economy Class. In case that something goes wrong, the captain, vice captain and flight attendants have totally different inflight meals.

The airplane meals should go through many procedures, from purchasing, primary processing, hot cooking and cold cooking to refrigeration and boarding, which need ten hours. But it expires six hours later, and would be abandoned once it gets out from the air food company for more than six hours.

飞机餐饮小八卦

在飞机上，不是什么食品都能吃的，要做到吃鱼不能有刺、吃肉不能有骨头。由于飞机在飞行过程中经常出现颠簸状况，这时旅客如果吃一些有硬物的食品或含有刺的鱼，容易噎住。

给同一个航班配餐，品种也有很大差异。头等舱与普通舱的饮食品种就很不同。为防止食品出现意外，正机长、副机长、机组乘务员吃的航空餐，也完全不同。

从采购、初加工、热厨、冷厨，再到冷藏、上飞机等，航空餐要经过多道程序，整个制作过程需要 10 小时，而保质期仅 6 小时！出了航空食品公司超过 6 小时就要报废。

案例分析

南航汕头航空有限公司为丰富旗下航班的机上经济舱餐食，通过以粤菜结合地方特色菜系的形式，推出了 45 款具有各地地方特色的菜品，让不同地域的旅客都能品尝到特有的餐食风味。

据介绍，南航在全国各地机场的配餐点共有 80 个。这 45 款地方特色菜品已陆续登上广州、北京、深圳等地的 15 个机场的部分出港航班经济舱，经济舱旅客也能吃到特色餐啦。为满足旅客选择多样性需求，这 45 款特色产品将按照每月更换的频率循环配供。

问题 请举例说明国内外航空公司机上餐饮服务的亮点。

参考答案

国泰航空的飞机餐充满了中国味。无论是凤梨酥甜点，还是餐后茶饮，无疑都特别符合国人的口味。

日本航空的飞机餐目前和摩斯汉堡、吉野家都有合作，还推出了超级可爱的"熊本餐"。

长荣航空最特别的是 Hello Kitty 餐，连餐巾纸上都是 Hello Kitty。不说口味，外观就迷倒一群少女心啦！

如果想品尝东南亚菜，亚洲航空一定是最好的选择，因为菜品实在太多了。但经济舱是不提供飞机餐的，如果提前在官网上预订，可享受折扣价，并且有几十种菜品可选！

Situation 13 Duty-Free Sales

任务单

主题：飞机飞行途中提供免税商品销售服务。请根据主题和必选项、可选项的要求，编写一段英文对话。

| 必选项 | 飞行途中提供免税商品销售服务 |

可选项
1. 乘务员询问旅客是否需要购买免税商品
2. 旅客主动询问是否有免税商品
3. 免税商品：化妆品 / 香水 / 酒 / 手表
4. 从免税品网站预购 / 在飞机上现购
5. 有货 / 售罄
6. 支付方式：现金 / 信用卡

典型对话

乘务员询问旅客是否需要购买免税商品

FA: Hello, would you like to buy some duty-free goods? We have a fine selection on board today.
您好！您需要购买一些免税商品吗？我们的商品都很不错呢。

P: Well, I'd like to buy a gift for my wife. Could you recommend something?
我想给我的妻子买一份礼物。您有什么推荐的吗？

FA: Sure. How about perfumes, cosmetics or silk scarves?
当然，香水、化妆品、丝巾都很合适，您觉得呢？

P: En. Let me see. Silk scarves, please.
呃，让我想想，丝巾吧。

FA: All right. How do you like this one with traditional design and bright color?
好的。您觉得这个如何？古典的设计，颜色也很亮。

P: Looks fine. Is it pure silk?
看上去不错。是真丝的吗？

FA: Yes. Guaranteed pure silk and made in Hangzhou, a city famous for silk.
是的，绝对是真丝，它是著名的丝绸之乡杭州生产的。

P: OK. How much is it?
好的，多少钱？

FA: 170 US dollars. How would you like to pay, cash or credit card?

170 美元。您是现金还是信用卡支付?

P: Would you accept traveler's check?

旅游支票可以吗?

FA: Sorry, we don't.

不好意思，我们不收支票。

P: That's all right. Here you are.

那好吧，现金给您。

FA: Thank you! Enjoy the flight!

谢谢! 祝您旅途愉快!

旅客主动询问免税商品

P: Excuse me, Miss.

您好，女士。

FA: Yes? May I help you?

有什么可以帮您的?

P: I have pre-ordered a lipstick from your online company site. When could I get it?

我在贵航空公司的网站预定了唇膏，我什么时候可以拿到?

FA: Well, could you show me the order number?

您的预定编号是多少?

P: Here it is.

是这个。

FA: Wait a moment. I will bring it to you.

请稍等，我给您拿过来。

P: Thanks!

谢谢!

FA: Here you are.

给您。

P: Looks great. Could I buy one more?

看上去挺好的。我可以再买一个吗?

FA: Sure. Cash or credit card?

可以。您是现金还是信用卡支付?

P: Cash. Here it is.

现金，给您。

FA: Here is your change.
这是找零。

高频语句

01 Is there anything I can do for you?
有什么能为您效劳的？
相关表达　May I help you?
　　　　　Do you need any help?

02 If you are interested in buying duty-free goods, you could have a look at our skyshop brochure in the seat pocket.
如果您有意购买免税商品，您可以翻看椅背口袋里我们航空商店的宣传册。
相关表达　If you'd like to buy some duty-free items, just read the brochure in the seat pocket.

03 Would you like to buy some duty-free goods? 您想购买免税商品吗？
相关表达　Do you sell duty-free items on board?

04 Can you recommend a perfume for a young girl?
您能推荐一款适合年轻姑娘用的香水吗？
相关表达　Can you give me some suggestions?

05 This particular item is currently out of stock.
这款特供商品现在缺货。
相关表达　This particular item is currently not available.
　　　　　The item you selected is currently sold out.

06 All the items are sold at marked price on the flight.
飞机上所有商品均按固定价格出售。
相关表达　Sorry that we can't give you any discount.

07 Here is your change.
这是找零。
相关表达　Keep the change.

专业词汇

duty-free goods (items) / catalogue　免税商品 / 商品目录

traveler's check / credit card / cash　　旅行支票 / 信用卡 / 现金

US dollars / UK pounds / Japanese yen / Chinese *yuan*　　美元 / 英镑 / 日元 / 人民币

exchange rate　　汇率

拓展知识

Duty-free goods on the plane

Nowadays, international airlines are usually selling duty-free goods on international flights in the course of the in-flight service, before the landing. Items sold on airplanes are duty-free and at a more affordable price. Sometimes, airlines will also get some exclusive product sets and preferential prices from the brand companies, so the price will be more attractive.

As we know, the duty-free goods on international air flights usually include cosmetics, perfume, jewelry, tobacco, alcohol and exclusive souvenirs of airlines. However, the airplanes have limited space and the duty-free goods are always on board in advance. Thus, there won't be too many varieties of items in the handcart when the flight attendants serve duty-free goods. What's more, each item may only have one or two pieces, and soon sell out. Passengers often have no chance to get what they take a fancy to. Airlines, therefore, have launched a new mode of online booking recently. For example, passengers may book what they like on the airline websites or via the dedicated WeChat or through the phone in the stated time prior to takeoff. And they would get it while On–board.

机上免税品

如今，全球各大航空公司的国际航班上都有机上免税品销售这一服务。通常是在国际航班起飞后一段时间到落地前，在机舱服务的过程中提供。在飞机上销售的货品卖点是"免税"，意味着价格更实惠。有时航空公司还会从品牌方获得一些独家在机上销售的产品套装和优惠价，因此价格会更具吸引力。

据了解，航空公司国际航班上的机上免税品通常包括彩妆保养品、香水、珠宝饰品、烟酒以及航空公司的独家纪念品等。但是通常因为机上空间有限，这些免税品都是提前上机的，所以空乘人员的售货小车上不会有太多品种和单品，每一种产品一般只有一两件，卖完即止，因此会出现看中了买不到的情况。对此，航空公司近年来推出了网上预订的销售方式，比如旅客可在搭乘航班前的规定时间内，在航空公司的网站和机上免税品销售的专门微信或电话中订购，在机上可取到货。

答疑解惑

机上免税品销售给航空公司带来利润的同时,也给旅客带来了各种实惠享受中高端品牌产品的机会。航空公司的网站上都会有机上免税品介绍,有的航空公司还会推出有独立域名的免税品官网,如南航、东航。

问题 请举例说明,国内外航空公司在机上免税品方面各自的优势与创新。

参考答案

1. 销售网站方面:南航和东航均有独立域名的免税品官网。南航网站最为漂亮;国航、东航网站较为简单;海航则和美兰机场免税店联营。

2. 货物配送方面:海航可以在机上选择免税品、填写购物单、离开海南岛时取货。在南航机上免税商城预订免税品,只要在广州机场机舱口选择提货服务,就可以享受"折上 9.6 折"的优惠。据了解,这种机舱口提货服务是南航机上免税商城针对国际旅客打造的便捷提货服务,预购免税品的旅客不必担心购买的产品因为体积重量和预订时间限制而无法配送上机。只要选择机舱口提货服务,就会有专人在旅客登机时提供一对一的配送服务,确保被预订的每一件商品都能在机舱口交付。不过,南航的这一服务目前只能在广州机场体验。

3. 产品方面:国航、东航以产品本身属性为分类,划分为化妆品、礼品、烟酒等类目;南航在此基础上增加了性别属性和功能属性的划分,如:精彩女人、魅力男士、共享欢乐等,使其更具个性化和人性化。南航免税店入驻品牌最多,产品最为丰富,且唯有南航推出了独家产品(虽然目前只有一款);产品最单一的为国航。

4. 预定途径方面:南航采取微信订购、在线订购等方式,航班起飞前 48 小时内可预订;国航、东航均是在正常工作日期间电话预订,例如东航规定至少在航班起飞前 72 小时内确认订单,才能确保配送到位。

5. 优惠活动方面:航空公司都有各自的会员卡,会员在每次飞行时都会在符合相应规定时获得里程累积的奖励。一些航空公司的会员里程卡的积分可在选购免税品时折现并可在结算时抵扣。有的航空公司则规定购买机上免税品也可以累积里程,如国泰和港龙航空规定"亚洲万里通"会员在购买机上免税品时可赚取"亚洲万里通"的里程数。

Landing
04 Scene

Situation 14　Landing Announcement, Farewell and Greeting

任务单

主题：飞机抵达目的地，乘务员进行客舱广播，告知旅客相关情况。请根据主题和必选项、可选项的要求，编写一段英文广播稿或对话。

必选项
1. 乘务员告知旅客飞机抵达目的地
2. 乘务员向旅客提醒注意事项

可选项
1. 广播 / 对话
2. 即将降落 / 正在滑行 / 已经停稳 / 延迟降落 / 转换到其他机场降落
3. 注意事项：安全带 / 电子设备 / 行李物品 / 座椅背 / 小桌板 / 遮阳板等
4. 航班 / 降落机场 / 航空公司等

典型对话

下降广播

　　Ladies and gentlemen, we will be landing at Shanghai Hongqiao Airport in about 30 minutes. Now we have started our descent, so please fasten your seat belt. Tray tables should be stowed. Seat backs should be returned to the upright position. Please do not use the lavatory. For passengers sitting by the windows, would you mind opening the window shades? Thank you!

　　女士们、先生们，本架飞机预计在约30分钟后到达上海虹桥机场。现在飞机已经开始下降高度，请您系好安全带，收起小桌板，调直座椅靠背。盥洗室暂停使用。坐在窗边的旅客，请将遮光板打开。谢谢！

乘务员告知旅客下机广播

Ladies and gentlemen, we have landed at the assigned position. Please check and take all your belongings with you. Take care when opening the overhead compartment. Get off one by one from the exit. Your baggage would be claimed in the terminal. Thank you for choosing Air China. Have a nice day. Thank you!

女士们、先生们，飞机已经停靠在指定位置。请您确认、携带好您的全部手提行李，小心开启行李架。依次从登机门下机。您的托运行李请到机场行李提取处领取。感谢您选择中国国际航空公司的班机，祝您旅途愉快，谢谢！

旅客尚未回座位

FA：Excuse me, Miss.

您好，女士。

P：Yes? What's the matter?

怎么了？

FA：We are about to land at the airport. Would you please return to your seat?

飞机即将降落，请您回到座位上。

P：I just want to go to the lavatory.

我想去盥洗室。

FA：Sorry, Miss. The lavatory has been suspended for the plane is landing.

不好意思，女士，飞机已经开始下降了，盥洗室已暂停使用。

P：Oh, all right.

哦，好的。

FA：Thanks! Please fasten your seat belt till the "Fasten Seat Belt" sign goes off.

谢谢！请一直系好安全带直到安全带指示灯关闭。

P：Get it. Thank you!

好的，谢谢！

旅客询问相关信息

P：Excuse me, Miss. May I ask you a question?

女士，您好！我可以问一个问题吗？

FA：Sure. What's it?

可以的，请问。

P：Are we arriving? We seem to have been circling for a while.

我们到了吗？我感觉似乎盘旋了有一会儿了。

FA: Well, as it's raining heavily at the airport at present, the visibility is a bit poor. We are waiting for the green light from the control tower.

因为目前机场大雨，能见度低，我们正在等待塔台的批准。

P: Will it be all right?

要不要紧啊？

FA: Don't worry. Everything goes fine. Please wait patiently.

别担心，没关系的。请耐心等待。

P: All right.

好的。

FA: Thank you for your understanding and cooperation.

谢谢您的理解和配合。

高频语句

01 We are about to land at Shanghai Pudong International Airport.

我们即将抵达上海浦东机场。

相关表达　We are going to land.

We shall be descending very soon.

02 The plane is going to arrive on schedule.

飞机将按时抵达目的地。

相关表达　Our arrival will be delayed due to the weather.

本次航班因天气原因将延迟抵达。

We should be arriving five minutes earlier than scheduled.

飞机会提前五分钟抵达。

03 Please don't unfasten your seat belt until the "Fasten Seat Belt" sign goes off.

当安全带指示灯熄灭后，再解开安全带。

相关表达　Please fasten your seat belt while the Fasten Seat Belt Sign is on.

Please keep your seat belt fastened until the plane has come to a complete stop.

04 Please don't turn on your mobile phone until you get off the plane.

下飞机前，请保持移动电话处于关机状态。

相关表达　Please keep your mobile phone off before getting off the plane.

⑤ Please check and take all your belongings with you.

请您检查是否带齐随身行李。

相关表达　Please make sure that you have taken all the baggage with you.

⑥ Please pull up the window shade.

请打开遮光板。

相关表达　Please return your seat to the upright position.

请调直座椅靠背。

Please fold your tray table up.

请收起小桌板。

⑦ Thanks for choosing China Eastern Airlines, and we are looking forward to serving you again.

感谢您乘坐东方航空公司班机，下次旅途再见。

相关表达　Thank you for selecting China Eastern Airlines for your travel today. Look forward to serving you again.

专业词汇

control tower　机场指挥塔台

domestic/international arrival hall　国内/国际到港大厅

terminal building　候机楼

domestic/international terminal　国内航班/国际航班候机楼

拓展知识

What does the flight atterdants have to do after the plane lands and the passengers leave?

When the plane lands on the stands with the arrival broadcast, the flight attendants will guide the passengers off the plane and provide necessary assistance. When all passengers get off the plane, the flight attendants will check the cabin once again to make sure there is no passenger detained or anything lost. The short-haul flights of AirAsia have the shortest transfer record for only 25 minutes. During this period, the flight attendants need to check for any non-operation items, fume in line with health and agricultural regulations and clean seats, so as to get ready for the passengers on the next flight.

飞机降落、旅客下机后，乘务人员还有哪些工作要做？

当飞机降落、抵达广播发出、飞机安全停靠在停机位后，乘务人员会引导旅客下机并提供必要协助。当所有旅客下机后，乘务人员会再次进行机舱检查以确保没有旅客滞留或有任何遗失物品。亚航短途航班曾仅耗时 25 分钟就完成了航班中转相关准备。在转场时间内，乘务人员需要检查是否有外来物品，熏蒸（以符合健康规定）、清洁座椅等，为迎接下一个航班的旅客做好准备。

案例分析

2015 年 5 月 28 日，北京首都国际机场一架开往广西南宁的航班在机坪上滑行，准备起飞。这时，旅客赵女士突然找到乘务员，称因航班延误了 40 分钟，耽误了她的预定行程，去了也白去，要求立即下飞机。经过沟通，机长同意赵女士下飞机。随后在地面空管允许情况下，飞机滑行准备推回机位。但在此过程中，赵女士不听乘务员安排，坚持离开自己的座位，要到飞机空着的前排舱位上就座，随后与乘务员发生口角冲突。

问题 遇到此类情况应如何应对？该旅客会受到处罚吗？

参考答案

鉴于上述情况，机长向地面报警。待飞机回到登机口后，机场派出所民警到场将赵女士传唤到派出所接受调查。因赵女士扰乱公共交通工具上的秩序，警方依据《治安管理处罚法》的相关规定，对其处以行政罚款 200 元。

民航法规规定，飞机自关闭舱门起即视为在飞行状态中，在机上的行为将受相关法律约束。在滑行准备起飞过程中，旅客应听从机组安排，以确保安全，切不可任性妄为，否则轻则耽误行程、面临治安处罚，重则将被追究刑事责任。

Situation 15 Transit / Connecting and Stopover Announcement

任务单

主题：飞机经停／转机，乘务员进行客舱广播，告知旅客相关情况。请根据主题和必选项、可选项的要求，编写一段英文广播稿或对话。

必选项
1. 乘务员告知旅客飞机抵达机场
2. 乘务员向旅客提醒注意事项

可选项
1. 广播／对话
2. 经停／转机
3. 注意事项：登机牌／行李／起飞时间等
4. 飞机按时抵达／延迟抵达
5. 正常转机／因飞机故障换乘飞机

典型对话

乘务员提醒经停旅客注意事项

Ladies and gentlemen, we are going to land at Beijing Capital International Airport. If you continue with the flight with us, please obtain your boarding pass from the transit lounge and wait for departure in the terminal. You may leave your baggage on the plane but take valuable belongings and important documents with you. The plane will stop here for one hour and ten minutes.

女士们、先生们，我们即将到达北京首都国际机场。经停的旅客请注意，请从地勤人员那里领取您的登机牌，并在候机楼等候。贵重物品和重要文件请您随身携带，其他行李可以留在飞机上。飞机预计在这里停留 1 小时 10 分钟。

经停旅客询问相关信息

P：Excuse me, Miss.
您好，女士。

FA：Yes. Can I help you?
有什么可以帮您的？

P：I didn't hear the announcement very clearly. As I just stop over here, could I stay on the plane?
刚刚的广播我没有听清。我只是经停，能在飞机上等候吗？

FA: I'm afraid not. All the passengers need to get off the plane.

恐怕不可以,所有旅客必须下飞机。

P: Oh, how about my baggage? Could I leave it on the plane?

啊,那我的行李怎么办?我能把它留在飞机上吗?

FA: Yes. But please take valuable belongings and important documents with you to the terminal.

可以的,但是贵重物品或重要文件请您随身携带至候机楼。

P: All right. How long should I wait at the airport?

好的。我需要在机场等多久?

FA: About an hour. There will be announcement for boarding. Please pay attention to it.

大约一小时。届时会有登机广播,请关注。

P: I see. Thank you very much.

我明白了,非常感谢。

FA: My pleasure.

不客气。

转机旅客询问相关信息

FA: Excuse me, Madam. Did you press the call button?

您好,女士。刚刚是您按的呼唤铃吗?

P: Yes. It seems that we are unable to arrive on schedule, right?

是的。我们是不是不能准点到达了?

FA: Yes. I'm afraid so. There is a heavy thunderstorm ahead of us. We may arrive 40 minutes later than the scheduled time.

是的,前方有强雷雨,我们可能要比预定时间晚40分钟。

P: Oh, I'm wondering whether I'll miss my connecting flight.

哦,我不知道我能否赶得上后面的转机航班了。

FA: When does your connecting flight expect to depart?

您的转机航班几点起飞?

P: An hour and a half later.

一个半小时后。

FA: Don't worry, Madam. We will contact the ground staff immediately. You will be informed as soon as we get the information about your subsequent flight.

别担心,女士,我们会马上帮您联系相关工作人员。关于您后续航班的情况,有消息会第一时间通知您。

P: All right. Thanks a lot!
好的,谢谢!

FA: You are welcome.
不客气。

高频语句

01 Please remain seated when the plane is still taxiing.
飞机还在滑行,请留在座位上。
相关表达　All passengers are required to remain seated before the plane comes to a stop.

02 Transit passengers proceed to the departure hall in the terminal building to arrange for your connecting flight.
需要转机的旅客,请您到候机楼出发大厅办理手续。
相关表达　If you have a connecting flight, you will have to go to the departure hall in the terminal building to arrange it.

03 The transit flight has been delayed until tomorrow. The airline will provide you with overnight accommodations.
转班飞机因故延误至明天。航空公司会为您安排住宿。
相关表达　The connecting flight has been cancelled today. We will be responsible for your accommodation tonight.

04 The departure time for the flight is 10:00 a.m.
飞机将在上午 10 点起飞。
相关表达　The flight will depart at 10:00 a.m.

05 We regret to announce that we have to transfer to another airplane due to a failure of engine.
很抱歉通知大家:由于发动机故障,我们将要换乘另一架航班。
相关表达　We are sorry to announce that we need to transfer to another flight because of a failure of engine.

06 It has been a pleasure serving you.
很荣幸为大家服务。
相关表达　We are delighted to be serving you.

专业词汇

direct flight
直达航班

stopover flight
经停航班

connecting / transit flight
中转航班

boarding bridge　廊桥，登机桥

拓展知识

Differences between direct flight, stopover flight and connecting flight

Types of flights	Meaning	Advantages	Disadvantages
Direct flight	Passengers need to check in only once directly from place A to B.	It's convenient, quick and simple.	Airfares are a little more expensive than those of other types of flights.
Stopover flight	If passengers leave place A for B, the airplane will stop over at place C for ground material rationing, such as food supply and refueling. The two sections are for the same airplane, and passengers from place A only need to get off at place C and board the plane again, without going out of the air terminal for security check again.	Airfares are moderate.	It may take some time to stop over but it won't take too long.

Types of flights	Meaning	Advantages	Disadvantages
Connecting flight	If passengers take a flight to place B, they need to get off the plane at place C and then transfer to another plane to place B. The two sections are for different airplanes in different flight numbers. And passengers from place A may have to go out of the air terminal for security check again.	Airfares are cheap and it can optimize the route to a greater extent.	The whole trip takes long and passengers sometimes need to stay overnight at the connecting place.

Notes: Better for passengers of connecting flights to bear in mind.

1. Connecting passengers should pay attention to the connecting time between flights when they buy tickets. The connecting time between domestic flights shall not be less than 2 hours, and the connecting time between domestic and international flights shall not be less than 3 hours.

2. If passengers transfer at regular airports, please try to take the luggage along as much as possible. Some airports have transfer counters, which can be used to handle boarding pass of the next section directly. But most of the counters cannot handle check-in luggage. If passengers have check-in luggage, you need to go to the luggage lobby to pick up the luggage, and then go to the departure lobby to re-check the boarding pass, and then go through security check.

3. In Beijing, Shanghai, Shenzhen and other large airports, the transfer and luggage check can be directly handled within the airport. After landing, passengers can ask the airport service personnel how to handle.

直飞、经停和中转航班的区别

航班类型	含义	优点	缺点
直飞航班	旅客从A地直接到达B地，只需要办理一次登机手续。	方便、快捷、简单。	票价较其他类型的航班稍贵。

航班类型	含义	优点	缺点
经停航班	旅客从A地始发,目的地为B地,中途停留在C地进行地面物资配给,如配餐食品供给、加油等。 两段航程乘坐相同的飞机,A地旅客只需在C地下机再重新登机一次即可,无需出候机楼重新过安检。	票价适中。	过站时会耽搁一些时间,但一般不会太久。
中转航班	旅客从A地乘坐某航班到B地,中途需要在C地下飞机并转乘另一个航班的飞机前往B地。 两段航程乘坐不同的飞机。旅客在C地下机后,可能需要出候机楼重新过安检。	票价便宜,可以较大程度优化航线。	整个航程时间较长,有时需要在转机地过夜。

备注:中转航班旅客注意事项

1. 转机旅客在购票时要注意航班之间的衔接时间,国内与国内航班衔接时间不得少于2小时,国内与国际航班衔接时间不得少于3小时。

2. 如果在普通机场中转,请尽量随身携带行李。有的机场在场内设有中转柜台,可以直接办理下段航班登机牌,但大多不能办理行李托运。如旅客有托运行李,需到行李大厅取行李,然后到出港大厅重新办理登机牌,再过安检。

3. 北京、上海、深圳等地的大型机场,在场内可直接办理中转及行李托运。飞机落地后,旅客可询问机场服务人员如何办理。

案例分析

哈尔滨机场行李发放员李晨发现,一位外籍旅客神色焦急地在行李提取厅来回踱步。他立即上前询问,得知该旅客需转机去往青岛,但是提取行李后,不知该如何办理转机手续。由于该旅客只会讲俄语,双方用英语沟通得并不顺畅,而转机时间只剩70分钟了。

问题 遇到这种情况,服务人员应如何处理?

李晨担心该旅客误机,立刻引导其到值机柜台办理转机手续,又引导其进行安检,一直将其送至登机口。该旅客得以顺利登机,哈尔滨机场工作人员热情周到的服务受到旅客称赞。

Passengers with Special Needs

Situation 16 Expectant Passengers

任务单

主题：乘务员与怀孕旅客确认孕周，并为其服务。请根据主题和必选项、可选项的要求，编写一段英文对话。

必选项
1. 询问旅客是否怀孕
2. 确认旅客孕周
3. 询问其有无家人陪伴
4. 为其提供特别关照服务

可选项
1. 孕周 32 周之内 / 孕周 32 周以上 35 周以下
2. 孕周 32 周以上 35 周以下的怀孕旅客持有 / 无医院医生开具的允许乘机的证明
3. 为孕妇提供枕头 / 毛毯 / 饮料等服务（注意饮料种类是否适合孕妇）

典型对话

迎客期间，乘务员与怀孕 25 周的旅客对话

FA: Good morning, lady. Are you pregnant?
女士您好，请问您是否已经有宝宝了？

P: Yes, I'm 25 weeks pregnant.
是的，我怀孕 25 周。

FA: Oh, congratulations! Here are the pillow and two blankets for you. Let me help you put the pillow around your waist, so that you will feel more comfortable. You can put one blanket around your belly, fasten the seat belt above it and cover your legs with the other one.
那太恭喜您啦，这是给您的一个枕头和两条毛毯，枕头我来帮您垫在腰上，这样在您休息的时候能舒服点。一条毛毯帮您垫在腹部，安全带帮您扣在上面，另一条给您盖在腿上。

P： Thank you very much!

谢谢您！

FA： You are welcome. If anything we can do for you, please press the call button above your head and I'll come to you as soon as possible. Have a good journey!

女士不客气。呼唤铃在您头顶上方，有任何需要可以随时叫我。我会第一时间赶来。祝您旅途愉快！

迎客期间，乘务员与怀孕 33 周的旅客对话

FA： Good morning, are you an expectant mother?

女士您好，请问您是否已经有宝宝了？

P： Yes.

是的。

FA： How many weeks are you pregnant?

请问您怀孕多少周？

P： More than 33 weeks.

已经 33 周了。

FA： Congratulations! Do you have a permit to fly by the doctor?

那太恭喜您啦！请问您有医生开具的可以乘坐飞机的证明吗？

P： Yes, wait a minute. But why do I need this proof?

有，我找下，不过为什么需要这个证明呢？

FA： According to CAAC regulations, passengers who are pregnant more than 32 weeks and less than 35 weeks should offer the proof of permission issued by the doctor. Thank you for you cooperation!

根据民航规定，32 周以上 35 周以下的孕妇乘机需持有医生出具的许可证明。谢谢您的配合！

饮料服务期间，乘务员与怀孕旅客对话

FA： Good morning, lady. We have coca cola, orange juice, apple juice, green tea and coffee. Which one do you prefer?

女士您好，我们供应的饮料有可乐、橙汁、苹果汁、绿茶和咖啡，请问您需要哪一种？

P： A cup of iced coke.

您好，我需要一杯冰可乐。

FA： Iced coke is not good for an expectant woman. Are you sure?

您现在怀有宝宝，确定可乐要加冰吗？

P： Alright. Please give me a cup of orange juice.

那也是，麻烦给我一杯橙汁吧。

FA: OK, just a moment.

好的，您稍等。

高频语句

01 There are lavatories in the front and rear of the cabin.

客舱的前部和后部都有洗手间。

相关表达　The lavatory is located in the front/rear of the cabin.

02 Let me help you put the pillow around your waist, so that you will feel more comfortable.

枕头我来帮您垫在腰上，这样在您休息的时候能舒服点。

03 If you have any need, please press the call button above your head and I'll come to you as soon as possible.

呼唤铃在您头顶上方，有任何需要可以随时叫我，我会第一时间赶来。

相关表达　Please don't hesitate to ask me for help whenever you need it.

04 Do you have a permit to fly by the doctor?

请问您有医生开具的可以乘坐飞机的证明吗？

05 According to CAAC regulations, expectant passengers who are pregnant more than 32 weeks and less than 35 weeks should offer the proof of permission issued by the doctor.

根据民航规定，32周以上35周以下的孕妇乘机需持有医生出具的许可证明。

06 Iced coke is not good for an expectant woman.

冰可乐对孕妇身体不好。

专业词汇

expectant passenger / expectant mother / pregnant woman　怀孕的旅客；孕妇

permission issued by the doctor

（孕妇）乘机许可证明

pillow and blanket   枕头和毛毯

lavatory / toilet   （机上）洗手间

拓展知识

The pregnant woman must comply with the conditions of traffic and can fly with the carrier's consent. Women who have been pregnant for less than 32 weeks can take the plane as the regular passengers except those who are diagnosed by the doctor as unfit for traveling by plane. Women who have been pregnant for 32 weeks and less than 35 weeks should have a medical license issued within one week prior to the flight.

For the following circumstances, pregnant women are not allowed to go through check-in procedures:

1. Women who have been pregnant for 35 weeks or more;

2. Pregnant women who are due within 4 weeks or less;

3. Pregnant women who are unable to determine the exact expected date of pregnancy;

4. Pregnant women who are known to have multiple births or expected to have complications with childbirth;

5. Parturient women for less than seven days after childbirth.

孕妇必须符合运输条件并且经承运人的同意方能乘坐飞机。怀孕不足 32 周的孕妇乘机，除医生诊断为不适合乘机外，按一般旅客运输。怀孕满 32 周且不足 35 周的孕妇乘机时，应当持有乘机前一周内签发的乘机医疗许可。

对于下列情况，一般不予办理乘机手续：

1. 怀孕 35 周及以上的孕妇；

2. 预产期在 4 周及以内的孕妇；

3. 无法确定准确预产期的孕妇；

4. 已知为多胎分娩或预计有分娩并发症者；

5. 产后不足 7 天的产妇。

案例分析

已有 9 个月身孕的冯女士在家人的陪伴下乘坐东航 MU2652 航班回老家待产。不料在飞行途中突然临产，机上乘务人员紧急处置：4 名空姐为其接生，机长紧急呼叫地面，飞机紧急备降武汉天河国际机场。最后婴儿顺利降生，母子平安。但所有乘务人员和当事人都紧张不已，多少有些后怕。

问题 航空公司为什么限制准妈妈乘飞机？

参考答案

在高空中，空气中的氧气相对减少、气压降低；飞机在起飞和降落时因海拔高度急剧变化引起大气压强差，容易引起人体不适。而孕妇的免疫系统处于相对较弱的状态，抗外界干扰能力差，更易引发不适。

医学认为，早孕期间（1 个月至 3 个月）胎盘没有完全发育成熟，相对容易流产，而航空旅行时飞机起降重力变化、气压变化、气流颠簸、晕机等都有可能增加流产概率。机场安检时的 X 线照射、高空较地面强 10 倍以上的宇宙辐射，以及核事故所泄漏的空中辐射悬浮物，都有可能影响早期胚胎而造成胎儿畸形。妊娠 7 个月以后容易发生早产、胎盘早剥、高血压、静脉炎，以及不慎摔倒或碰撞，这些都会增加母体或胎儿发生意外的概率。因此，早孕期间和妊娠 7 个月以上不宜乘坐飞机。

孕妇在飞行途中容易发生早产、流产、胎儿宫内缺氧等意外事故，而飞机上缺乏相应的医疗设备，一旦出现意外情况，后果不堪设想。

航空公司对孕妇搭乘飞机的限制或规定，既是出于对孕妇及胎儿安全的考虑，也是为了维护其他旅客以及航空公司的利益。孕妇乘坐飞机，若在飞行过程中发生意外，出于安全考虑，飞机必须降落至最近的机场送其接受医疗，这就会造成当次航班的延误，甚至影响到后续一系列的航班，既影响到众多旅客的出行，也会给航空公司造成巨大的经济损失。

Situation 17　Passengers with Infants

任务单

主题：乘务员为携带婴儿乘机的旅客服务。请根据主题和必选项、可选项的要求，编写一段英文对话。

必选项	1. 主动提供并介绍婴儿安全带的使用方法，协助旅客帮婴儿系好安全带 2. 介绍洗手间的位置及内有婴儿护理板，有需要时可以使用 3. 婴儿哭闹，帮助其有针对性地解决问题
可选项	1. 婴儿因为饥饿/尿布潮湿而哭泣 2. 旅客自身携带/未携带奶粉、奶瓶或尿不湿 3. 冲泡奶粉的要求自行设定：100ml/120ml/150ml 4. 需要/不需要为旅客提供婴儿摇篮

典型对话

携带婴儿的旅客登机，乘务员提供和介绍安全设备

FA: Hello, lady. Would you like me to take a baby seat belt for you?
女士，您好！需要我帮您拿一条婴儿安全带吗？

P: Sure. Thanks! But I don't know how to use it.
好的，谢谢！可是我不会使用。

FA: Let me help you. First, we can insert one end of the seat belt into the circular socket of baby seat belt. Second, fasten your seat belt. Last, fasten baby seat belt around your baby. That's it!
我来帮助您。首先，我们把座椅上的安全带小头绑在婴儿安全带的圆形插孔里；然后，您先系好安全带；最后将婴儿安全带系在宝宝身上。这样就可以了！

P: Ok, thank you very much!
好的，谢谢！

FA: My pleasure.
乐意效劳。

乘务员帮助婴儿母亲冲泡奶粉

FA: Good morning, lady. The baby is crying. Would you like some assistance?
　　女士您好，宝宝一直在哭，我可以帮助您吗？

P: I'm sorry about the noise. I think he is hungry.
　　很抱歉打搅大家，我想他一定是饿了。

FA: Have you taken powdered milk with you? Can I help you with the powdered milk?
　　您携带奶粉了吗？需要我帮您冲泡吗？

P: Yes, the powdered milk is in my bag. Could you please give me a hand? Two teaspoons of milk powder, 150 ml. Thank you!
　　我包里带了奶粉。能否麻烦你帮忙冲泡一下，两勺奶粉，150ml。谢谢！

FA: Of course. Please wait a minute.
　　当然可以，请您稍等。

用餐期间，乘务员与携带婴儿的旅客对话

FA: Hello, Madam. This is the baby meal you ordered.
　　女士您好，这是您预订的婴儿餐。我帮您拿过来。

P: OK. Can you tell me something about it?
　　好的，你能帮我介绍一下吗？

FA: Yes, this is a customized rice paste for airlines. How about its temperature?
　　这是航空公司定制的米糊辅食。您看温度还可以吗？

P: It's OK. Thanks!
　　好的，谢谢！

高频语句

01 Please hold your baby outside the seat belt. I will get you a baby seat belt.
　　请将婴儿放在安全带外，我给您取一条婴儿安全带。
　　相关表达　Would you like me to take a baby seat belt for you?
　　　　　　　Would you like to have a longer seat belt for you?

02 If you want to change the baby diaper, you can go to the lavatory.
　　您可以去洗手间给宝宝换尿布。
　　相关表达　You can use the changing board in the lavatory, if your baby need to change his diaper.

③ We have some extra diapers. Which size does he wear?

机上备有纸尿裤，请问他穿什么尺寸？

④ We have a baby bassinet on board.

机上备有婴儿摇篮。

相关表达　There are baby bassinets on board, but they are all booked.

⑤ He may feel more comfortable with a pacifier.

他如果吮吸奶嘴可能更舒适些。

⑥ Please be sure not to leave him unattended.

请不要让他离开您的视线。

专业词汇

baby seat belt　婴儿安全带

baby bassinet　婴儿摇篮

baby meal　婴儿餐

pacifier/soother　安抚奶嘴

拓展知识

A baby passenger is a baby for 14 days to 2 years old. For domestic flights, baby tickets are usually sold at 10% of the adult's full fare of the same flight with no seats and no free baggage allowance, and free to bring only a bassinet or a pushchair. Babies should buy children's tickets if they need separate seats. If an adult passenger has more than one infant, only one can pay 10% of the total fare of the adult, and the rest should buy children's tickets at 50% of the adult's full fare. According to the relevant provisions of Civil Avaiation Law of the People's Republic of China, baby passenger must be accompanied by an adult when taking the plane, and they should not sit in emergency exits rows. In case seats in the same row are all occupied, no more than one baby passenger is allowed in that row. A baby born less than 14 days or a premature infant less than 90 days old is usually not allowed to take the plane.

婴儿旅客是指出生14天至2周岁的婴儿。国内航班通常按照同一航班成人普通票价的10%购买婴儿票，不提供座位、无免费行李额，仅可免费携带一摇篮或可折叠式婴儿车。如婴儿需要单独占座位时，应购买儿童票。如每位成人旅客所带婴儿超过一个，只有一个可按成人全票价的10%付费，其余按成人全票价的50%购买儿童票。根据《中华人民共和国民用航空法》的相关规定，婴儿旅客乘坐飞机时必须有成人陪伴，并且不得坐在紧急出口的位置。相连的同一排座位上都有旅客时，不得出现两个不占座的婴儿。出生不足14天的婴儿或出生不足90天的早产儿通常不予承运。

案例分析

2015年9月23日，在一架从喀什飞往上海虹桥的飞机上，一位怀抱婴儿的妇女突然从座位上站起来，面色惊慌地哭喊："我要下飞机！"原来，这位妇女的孩子仅两个月大，在飞机起飞5分钟后，婴儿突然面色苍白、呼吸骤停。在机舱乱作一片的时候，四位医生立刻站出来，毫不犹豫地施救。40分钟后，返航的飞机落地，孩子被送进急救病房。但遗憾的是，孩子终因病情过重，没能救过来。

问题 多大的婴儿可以乘坐飞机？

参考答案

航空公司规定，出生14天以上、身体健康的婴儿才可以搭乘飞机。由于新生儿肺部尚未完全张开，毛细血管脆弱，身体对气压、重力等因素变化的耐受力较弱，因此14天内的新生儿不宜乘机。最好等宝宝4~6周以后再带其飞行。家长还要注意，上机前不宜让宝宝吃得太饱，还要保证没有发烧症状，鼻腔必须通畅。

即使宝宝已满符合坐飞机的年龄，但要宝宝长期待在机舱里面，难免会有点小无聊，如果在飞机里哭闹，家长会非常尴尬。还要考虑到宝宝的食物、保暖、护理等问题，要提前给宝宝准备好周全的物品哦！

Situation 18 Unaccompanied Minor

任务单

主题：乘务员与无人陪伴儿童对话，并为其服务。请根据主题和必选项、可选项的要求，编写一段英文对话。

必选项
1. 确认其目的地
2. 乘机有效证件的安放以及随身和托运行李的件数
3. 主动为无人陪伴小旅客介绍服务设施，指导其系好/解开安全带
4. 沟通是否有晕机现象
5. 询问儿童冷暖情况，为其增添衣物
6. 去洗手间，乘务员确认其回到原座位并系好安全带
7. 飞机下降时，唤醒睡着的无人陪伴儿童，防止耳压
8. 下机时，乘务员嘱咐无人陪伴小旅客不擅自离开，等待乘务员送行

可选项
1. 根据机上条件提供适合的玩具和读物
2. 为无人陪伴儿童提供饮料和餐食，必要时为其分餐

典型对话

迎客期间，乘务员与无人陪伴儿童沟通是否曾经有晕机现象

FA：(The flight attendant crouches and communicates with unaccompanied child) Bob, how many times have you flown?

（乘务员蹲下与无人陪伴的儿童沟通）鲍勃，这是你第几次坐飞机呀？

P：Miss, I've solely traveled by air for about three times.

阿姨好，我已经单独坐了3次飞机了。

FA：So cool. Did you get upset when you were flying?

这么厉害！你之前坐飞机的时候有不舒服吗？

P：Yes, I always feel like vomiting during takeoff and descending.

有的，阿姨，起飞和下降的时候老想吐。

FA：Here are clean bags for you, you can put them in the chair pocket in front of you. If you feel uncomfortable, please don't hesitate to press the call button which is above your head. I will come as soon as possible.

阿姨多给你几个清洁袋放在前面椅子的口袋里。有任何不舒服的情况记得按呼唤铃，呼唤铃就在头顶上面。阿姨看到马上就会过来的。

P：Thank you, Miss!

谢谢阿姨！

飞机在地面延误时，乘务员与无人陪伴儿童对话

FA：Hi, do you have a mobile phone with you?

小朋友，你有手机吗？

P：No.

没有啊。

FA：Well, your mother will come to meet you, right? Our plane will be delayed for about an hour. I want to call your mother, so that she won't be worried about it. Do you remember her phone number?

飞机落地后，你妈妈来接你，对吗？我们的飞机可能延误一小时，阿姨用手机跟你妈妈打个电话，让她不要担心。你记得妈妈的电话号码吗？

P：Yes, it is 13813812345.

记得，是13813812345。

FA：OK.（The flight attendant should call his mother after checking the telephone number with the UM files）

好的。（跟信息档案核实无误后，与无人陪伴儿童的联系人取得电话联系）

高频语句

01 May I help you put your small back bag into the overhead compartment?

需要我帮你把小背包放进行李架吗？

02 We have comic books.

我们有漫画书。

03 I can tell you a story.

我可以给你讲一个故事。

04 Open the door of the lavatory like this. Be careful, don't hurt your hands.

这样子打开洗手间的门，小心点，别弄伤手。

05 This is child meal for you. Take care. It is hot.

这是你的儿童餐，当心烫。

06 Did you get upset when you were flying?

你之前坐飞机的时候有不舒服吗？

专业词汇

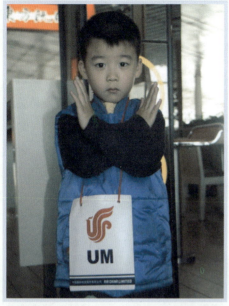

unaccompanied minor / unaccompanied child
无人陪伴儿童

child packs　　儿童玩具包

child meal　　儿童餐

clean / sick / waste bag　　清洁袋

拓展知识

　　Unaccompanied children usually refer to the children who are above (including) five years old and below twelve years and have to take the flight alone without the company of an eighteen-year-old adult with capacity for civil conduct. In domestic flights, children's tickets are usually sold at 50% of the adult's regular fare on the same flight, and children enjoy the same free baggage allowance as adults. In the international flights, different companies have different requirements on unaccompanied children's fare. Different types of aircrafts have different restrictions on the number of unaccompanied children. Therefore, unaccompanied children need to apply in advance, and submit materials such as identity cards and household registers to the airlines. Ground service personnel and flight attendants will take careful attention to unaccompanied children, which will be recorded in the file of unaccompanied children's file bags. Unaccompanied children who are under 5 years old are usually not allowed to take the flight.

　　无人陪伴儿童通常是指 5 周岁（含）以上、12 周岁以下的，并且在乘机过程中没有年满 18 周岁具有民事行为能力的成人陪伴，需要单独乘机的儿童。国内航班通常按照同一航班成人普通票价的 50% 购买儿童票，享有与成人相同的免费行李额，在国际航段上各个公司关于无人陪伴儿童的票价有着不同的规定。由于不同机型对于无人陪伴儿童的数量有着不同的限制，因此无人陪伴儿童需要提前申请乘机，并且向航空公司提交身份证、户口本等材料。地服人员和空乘人员会为无人陪伴儿童提供细致关照，并记录在无人陪伴儿童文件袋的相关档案中。不满 5 周岁的无人陪伴儿童通常不予承运。

案例分析

　　暑运旺季，经常有无人陪伴儿童乘机。北京至哈尔滨的东航 MU2717 航班乘务组就迎来了一位无人陪伴小旅客。客舱经理在与地面人员交接后，了解到这是一名既可爱又腼腆的七岁小女孩。

 请分析一下针对无成人陪伴儿童的个性化服务包含哪些内容。

参考答案

　　一路关爱一路情：乘务员吴婷婷一手帮无陪小旅客拿包，一手牵着她到指定座位上坐好，又给她小毛毯和靠垫，并轻声询问她是不是第一次坐飞机，随后耐心地为她介绍有关设备的使用方法。安顿好小旅客后，乘务员和所在区域的组员进行了沟通，以便对小旅客进行持续关注。

　　由于是雷雨季节，航班发生延误情况。考虑到小女孩是第一次独自乘坐飞机，难免会紧张，乘务员将准备好的折纸送给她。女孩收到后很高兴，紧张情绪有所缓和，等待也变得不再煎熬。

　　乘务员一路上主动询问小旅客喝不喝水、陪她轻声聊天，给予密切关注。对于乘务员们的关爱，小旅客开始不再腼腆，有时甚至主动找乘务员姐姐说话。时间过得很快，快到达目的地时，乘务员告诉小旅客飞机开始下降，并帮她系好安全带。

　　照顾单独乘机的小旅客是乘务组日常工作的一部分，乘务人员应让小旅客们感受到更多温暖与关爱。

Situation 19　Disabled Passengers

任务单

主题：乘务员主动为视觉障碍旅客提供服务。请根据主题和必选项、可选项的要求，编写一段英文对话。

必选项
1. 引导视觉障碍旅客入座
2. 向视觉障碍旅客介绍机上设施（不介绍阅读灯）
3. 向听说障碍旅客提供乘机安全温馨提示卡片
4. 以钟表指示方式向视觉障碍旅客介绍餐食
5. 飞机降落前，跟感官障碍旅客确认引导其下机的时间，让其耐心等待

可选项
1. 感官障碍旅客类型可自主设定为视觉障碍/行动障碍等
2. 轮椅旅客需要/不需要更换客舱内轮椅
3. 障碍旅客能够在客舱内自行走动/无法在客舱内自行走动
4. 担架旅客等特殊情况

典型对话

乘务员引导视觉障碍旅客入座

FA: How are you, Sir? Your seat number is 20C. Please take my shoulder. I'll show you to your seat.

先生，您好！您的座位在20C，请您搭着我的肩膀，我带您到座位上。

P: Fine, thank you!

好的，谢谢！

FA: This is your seat. Would you mind sitting down?（The flight attendant should guide the passenger gently.）

这是您的座位，请坐。（引导动作轻缓。）

FA:（Hold the hand of the blind passenger to touch the button）Sir, the lavatory is at the back of the cabin. This is the air conditioner knob on top of your head, and you can rotate it to adjust the air conditioning. This button next to it is a call bell. If you have any needs, please press the button and let us assist you.

（拉着视觉障碍旅客的手触摸按钮）先生，盥洗室在客舱的后部。您头顶上方的这个是空调旋钮，您可以左右旋转来调节空调大小。旁边的这个按钮是呼唤铃，如果您有任何需要，请随时按铃让我们帮助您。

P: Thank you!
　　谢谢!

就餐期间，乘务员与视觉障碍旅客对话

FA: Hello, Sir, you ordered rice with chicken, right?
　　先生，您好，您点的是鸡肉米饭，对吗？

P: Yes.
　　是的。

FA: OK. The fork is in your three o'clock direction. The six o'clock direction is today's staple rice with chicken. At your nine o'clock, it is mushroom soup. I'll open the tin foil for you. Please be careful.
　　好的。叉子在您的三点钟方向，六点钟方向是今天的主食鸡肉米饭，九点钟方向是蘑菇汤。我帮您把上面的锡纸打开，请您小心用餐。

P: It is very kind of you. Thank you.
　　你真好，谢谢你。

FA: You are welcome.
　　乐意效劳。

飞机降落前，乘务员与视觉障碍旅客对话

FA: Good afternoon, Sir. Our plane is about to land. After the plane has stopped, please wait for a while. I will come and take you down.
　　先生，您好，我们的飞机即将着陆。飞机停稳后，请您耐心等待一会儿，我会过来带您下飞机的。

P: OK, thank you.
　　好的，谢谢。

高频语句

01 We can assist you if you would like to go to the lavatory.
　　如果您想去洗手间，我们可以帮助您。

02 You have to change the special wheelchair on board.
　　您可能需要更换机上专用轮椅。

03 We are entering the cabin now. Please hang on to your chair.
　　我们现在进入客舱，请您坐稳扶好。

④ The fork is in your three o'clock direction. The six o'clock direction is today's staple chicken rice. At your nine o'clock, it is mushroom soup.

叉子在您的三点钟方向，六点钟方向是今天的主食鸡肉米饭，九点钟方向是蘑菇汤。

相关表达　May I introduce the meal for you? Salad is at three o'clock direction.

我能为您介绍一下饭食吗？沙拉在您的三点钟方向。

⑤ I'll open the tin foil for you. Please be careful.

我帮您把上面的锡纸打开，请小心用餐。

⑥ I'm afraid the seeing eye dog / guide dog can't take a passenger seat.

对不起，导盲犬不能单独占座。

专业词汇

blind passenger　视觉障碍旅客　　　　seeing eye dog　导盲犬
passenger in wheelchair　轮椅旅客　　　STCR　担架旅客

拓展知识

The physically or mentally challenged passengers refer to the passengers who cannot take care of themselves on their own due to physical or mental defects, mainly including blind passengers, deaf/dumb passengers, wheelchair passengers, stretcher passengers and psychiatric patients. The physically or mentally challenged passengers should fill in "the Application Form for Special Passenger Transportation" in advance, and if it is difficult for them to write, it may be written by others and signed by their guardians or relatives. When taking the flight, they shall also provide "the Certificate of Diagnosis for the Flight" within the period of validity (usually 96 hours before departure) provided by the medical institutions above the county level. Due to physical or mental inconvenience, the physically or mentally challenged passengers tend to have strong self-esteem and emotional instability, and are prone to be anxious. Therefore, when the flight attendants provide service to those passengers, they should do their best to help them travel safely and smoothly on the premise of protecting their self-esteem.

身心障碍旅客通常指在乘坐飞机中由于身体或精神的障碍，不能自行照料自己的旅客。主要包括视觉障碍旅客、听说障碍旅客、轮椅旅客、担架旅客、精神障碍旅客等。身心障碍旅客应提前填写《特殊旅客运输申请表》，如本人书写困难，可由他人代写，由监护人或亲属签字。

乘机时，还应提供有效期内（通常为起飞前96小时）县级以上医疗机构提供的《适飞诊断证明书》。由于身体或精神的不便，身心障碍旅客通常自尊心较强、情绪不稳定，容易产生焦虑情绪，因此空乘人员在针对身心障碍旅客提供服务时，应当在保护旅客自尊的前提下，竭尽所能帮助其平安顺利地度过旅程。

案例分析

23名身体障碍旅客从青岛坐飞机回重庆，其中两人完全无自理能力，需坐轮椅，另有四人需要拐杖。但他们没按规定提前申报，航空公司也没有提前做准备。为了让他们顺利登机，青岛流亭国际机场、西部航空公司、重庆机场等部门紧急协调，飞机从原定远机位更改为靠桥机位，并提前10分钟让他们登机，航空公司还从重庆派出一名男乘务员到青岛为他们服务。

问题 身心障碍旅客乘坐飞机前需注意什么？

参考答案

一架航班对身心障碍旅客有人数规定：航班座位数为51~100个的，不得超过2名（含2名）；航班座位数为101~200个的，不得超过4名（含4名）；航班座位数为201~400个的，不得超过6名（含6名）；航班座位数为400个以上的，不得超过8名（含8名）。载运身心障碍旅客人数超过上述规定时，应按1∶1的比例增加陪伴人员，但身心障碍旅客人数最多不得超过上述规定的一倍。载运身心障碍旅客团体（10人以上，含10人）时，在增加陪伴人员的前提下，可酌情增加身心障碍旅客乘机人数。

身心障碍旅客乘机前要填写《乘机申请书》，还要在购票及办理乘机手续时交验《诊断证明书》，由县级以上医院出具证明，证明其不需要额外医疗协助就可完成乘机。旅客必须在航班离站48小时前提出申请并得到航空公司给予承运的答复，然后在该航班开始办理乘机手续1小时前到航空公司值机柜台办理乘机手续。

Situation 20 Senior Passengers

任务单

主题：乘务员主动为老年旅客服务。请根据主题和必选项、可选项的要求，编写一段英文对话。

必选项
1. 主动为老年旅客指引座位
2. 协助老年旅客提拿、放置行李
3. 为其提供毛毯
4. 简单、大声地向其介绍设备

可选项
1. 简单了解其身体状况
2. 观察老年旅客携带/未携带拐杖
3. 帮助携带拐杖的老年旅客妥善放置拐杖
4. 目的地温度较高/较低，飞机下降期间提醒老年旅客增减衣物

典型对话

迎客期间，乘务员与70岁的老奶奶对话

FA：Hello, Madam. May I have a look at your boarding pass, please?

奶奶，您好，方便看一下您的登机牌吗？

P：Sure, here you are.

当然，给你。

FA：Madam, your seat is in 15A. I'll show you. Let me help you with your luggage.

奶奶，您的座位在15A，我带您过去。行李我来帮您拿。

P：Thank you, girl.

谢谢你，小姑娘。

FA：This is your seat. Please have a seat. Would you like to put your luggage on the overhead compartment or under the seat?

这是您的座位，您请坐。行李我是帮您放到行李架上还是座椅下方呢？

P：Just put it under the seat.

就放在座椅下方吧。

FA：OK. Let me help you.

好的，我来帮您。

FA: (After a while) Madam, this is the blanket for you. I'd like to cover it for you. You may push the button to control your chair after the flight takes off, so that you will feel more comfortable. The washroom is in the rear of the cabin. If you need any help, please press the call button and let me know.

（一会儿过后）奶奶，这是给您的毛毯，我来帮您盖上。飞机起飞后，您可以按下这个按钮来调整座椅靠背，这样会更舒适一些。洗手间在客舱后部。有任何需要请按一下呼唤铃，随时让我知道。

飞机下降期间，提醒老年旅客增减衣物

FA: Hello, Madam, the plane is about to decline. The temperature in Harbin is 10 degrees centigrade. You might feel cold. Do you have a coat in your carry-on? Would you like me to take it out for you?

奶奶您好，飞机即将下降。哈尔滨的温度是10摄氏度，比较凉爽。您的随身行李里有外套吗，需要拿给您披一下吗？

P: Yes, there is a coat in my bag. You can find it easily after opening the bag.

好的，在我的行李包里有一件外套，拉开行李包就能看到。

FA: (Find the coat) Let me help you with it.

（找出外套）我来帮您披上吧。

高频语句

01 Let me help you with your luggage.
我来帮您拿行李。

02 May I put the crutches under your seat?
我可以帮您把拐杖放到您座位下方吗？

03 You may push the button to control your chair.
您可以按这个按钮来调整座椅。
相关表达　You may push the button on the armrest to lean back your seat.

04 If you feel cold, you can turn the knob above your head. You can shut it off by turning it to the right.
如果您觉得冷，可以调节座椅上方按钮，向右旋转按钮可关闭。
相关表达　If you feel cold, you can turn it to the right to shut off.

05 Madam, this is the blanket for you.
女士，这是给您的毛毯。

06 The temperature in Harbin is 10 degrees centigrade. You might feel cold. Do you have a coat in your carry-on? Would you like me to take it out for you?

哈尔滨的温度是10摄氏度，比较凉爽。您的随身行李里有外套吗，需要拿给您披一下吗？

相关表达　It is very cold outside. Please dress warmly before going out.

专业词汇

carry-on　随身行李

temperature　温度

senior passenger　老年旅客

crutch　拐杖

拓展知识

Aged passengers usually refer to male passengers over 60 years old or female passengers over 55 years old who apply for the reception as aged passengers. If the aged passenger is in good health and has not made an application, he or she may take the plane as the ordinary passenger. It is important to note that, according to the relevant provisions issued by the Civil Aviation Administration of China, aged passengers over 70 years old must show "the certificate of diagnosis for the flight" issued by the medical institutions above the county level when taking the flight. Airports and airlines would take some special care of and provide special services for aged passengers.

老年旅客通常指年龄超过60周岁的男性或年龄超过55周岁的女性、并申请按照老年旅客接待的旅客。如果身体状况良好、未提出申请，可以按照普通旅客承运。需要特别注意的是，根据中国民航总局颁布的相关规定，70周岁以上的老年旅客在乘坐飞机时，必须出示县级以上医疗机构开具的《适飞诊断证明书》。机场和航空公司针对老年旅客都有一些专门关怀和特色服务。

案例分析

李先生准备和家人前往越南自助游。购买机票后接到航空公司的通知，要求他提供近一个月的心电图和血压结果证明。为了开证明，李先生折腾了很久。他先是跑到家旁边的社区医院，得知只能开具心电图证明，血压证明开不了。接着他又得知，航空公司对开证明的医院也有要求，必须是县级以上甲等医院。换了一家医院，又费了一番周折，李先生总算达到了航空公司的要求。

事后想了想，李先生有点纳闷。年初他乘坐过一次飞机，当时航空公司并没有这项要求。李先生即将搭乘飞机的航空公司还告诉他，乘机当天机场安检会进行抽检，他还是有点担心。

问题 老年旅客乘坐飞机是否需要出具健康证明？

参考答案

对于老年人乘坐飞机，不同的航空公司有不同的规定。南方航空公司对旅客年龄没有限制，只要老年人身体健康、能够自由上下飞机，是不需要开具证明的。北部湾航空公司则要求，60岁以上的旅客需提供县级以上医院出具的健康证明。老年旅客自行购票或代买者购票时，应事先了解各航空公司对此的规定。

Situation 21 Sickness

任务单

主题：乘务员与生病旅客对话，帮助其减轻病痛。请根据主题和必选项、可选项的要求，编写一段英文对话。

必选项	1. 旅客有不适症状 2. 了解其不适原因，有针对性地提供温水、毛巾、口香糖、晕机药、感冒药、止痛药、退烧药等 3. 有 / 无陪同人员 4. 有 / 无病史 5. 有 / 无随身携带药品
可选项	1. 旅客晕机 / 耳压 / 头痛 / 胃痛 / 发烧 2. 对于病情较重者，客舱广播寻找医生 3. 根据病情做出判断，必要时申请备降并提前联系地勤安排好医疗人员

典型对话

一名旅客感到不舒服，有反胃、耳朵不适的症状

P: Hello, I don't feel very well. I have an earache.
你好，我觉得不太舒服，耳朵疼痛。

FA: The pain in your ears is due to the change of air pressure. It is very common during the flight.
您感觉到耳朵不舒服是因为气压的变化，这在飞行中属于常见现象。

P: Ok, what should I do? Will it continue this way until the plane lands?
怎么办？会一直这样持续到飞机降落吗？

FA: Don't worry. You can just relieve the earache by chewing gums or swallowing. Would you like some gums?
别担心，您可以通过咀嚼口香糖或吞咽口水来缓解耳压。需要我拿几片口香糖给您吗？

P: OK.
好的。

FA: Try it, and you'll be better soon.
您尝试一下，一会儿就会好些了。

旅客晕机

FA: What can I do for you, Sir?

有什么可以帮助您的吗，先生？

P: Yes, I have a stomachache and feel like vomiting.

是的，我觉得胃不太舒服，有点想要呕吐。

FA: Is this your flight for the first time?

您是第一次乘坐飞机吗？

P: Yes.

是的。

FA: I'm afraid you have a bit airsickness.

恐怕您有些晕机。

P: But I don't have carsickness.

可是，我此前并不晕车啊。

FA: Some passengers are airsick, although they are not carsick or seasick.

有不少旅客不晕车、不晕船，但是会晕机呢。

P: OK. Is there any airsickness medicine on the plane?

好吧，飞机上提供晕机药吗？

FA: Sorry, we don't offer any airsickness medicine. I'll give you some more airsickness bags. There is a row of vacant seats in the rear of the cabin. You can have a rest there. Would you like a cup of warm water and hot towels?

不好意思，航班上没有晕机药。我多给您几个清洁袋。飞机后部有一整排座椅是空着的，您可以到那边休息。再给您一杯温开水和热毛巾可以吗？

FA: (After a while) Sir, this is a cup of warm water and hot towels.

（过了一会儿）先生，这是温开水和热毛巾。

P: Thank you! Would you please give me a glass of iced water? I'm a little thirsty.

谢谢！可以多给我一杯冰水吗？我有些口渴。

FA: Certainly, but maybe warm water is more suitable. Drink it, and you may feel more comfortable.

可以，不过温开水也许更合适些，您会觉得更舒适点。

P: Yes, you are very thoughtful.

好的，你很周到。

> 高频语句

01 What's the matter, Sir? You don't look very well.

先生，您怎么了？您好像不太舒服。

相关表达　You look pale.

02 Don't worry. That was because of a change in air pressure. You can relieve your earache by swallowing and by eating sweets. And then you'll feel better when the plane stops climbing.

请不要担心，这是由于大气压力的改变造成的，您可以通过吞咽口水和吃糖果来缓解耳痛。当飞机停止爬升时，您就会好些了。

相关表达　We should swallow or chew the chewing gum to balance the pressure to reduce the harm to ears.
　　　　　The change in cabin pressure would make his ears uncomfortable. Sucking on a soother might help your baby relieve the discomfort.

03 Don't worry. Here's a cup of hot water. You'll be all right.

请别担心，这是一杯热水，您马上就会好的。

相关表达　I suggest a glass of hot water. It may settle down your stomach.

04 Have you ever felt your heart uncomfortable? Do you bring any medicine with you? Do you have someone traveling with you?

您以前有感觉心脏不舒服吗？您有没有随身携带药物？有同行的人吗？

05 This is the pill for airsick, and this is a hot towel. I suggest you put it on your head and have a rest. Maybe you will feel better.

这是晕机药，这是热毛巾，我建议您把它放在额头上休息一下，您会稍微舒服一些。

06 Keep your arm up. Let's go to wash the cuts. Take it easy. The bleeding is controlled. I'll wrap it up with gauze.

抬高手臂，清洗一下伤口。不要紧张，血已经止住了，我用纱布将伤口包扎起来。

07 I'll go and see if there is a doctor on board.

我去看看机上是否有医生。

相关表达　I will make an announcement to see if there are some doctors on board.

08 I'm sorry to tell you there is no doctor on board. We've informed the ground staff and you'll be sent to the hospital as soon as the plane lands.

很抱歉，机上没有医生。但是我们已经通知地面人员，飞机一着陆，就会送您去医院。

相关表达　If you need to meet a doctor, we can contact with the ground to arrange for you in advance.

专业词汇

airsick　晕机	vomit　呕吐
shock　休克	chewing gum　口香糖
heart attack　心脏病发作	first aid treatment　急救治疗

拓展知识

Airsickness, similar to car sickness and sea sickness, is common among airline passengers. Passengers who are slightly airsick may have dizziness, chest tightness and other mild symptoms. Those who are severely airsick may look pale, keep vomiting and have abnormal sweating. Airsick symptoms are usually obvious during the takeoff and landing, turbulences and climbing of the airplane. Once the passengers have the airsick symptoms, flight attendants should take the initiative to care, help, and comfort with patience and provide a few more cleaning bags, hot towels and warm boiling water. It is important to note that airlines usually do not take the initiative to provide medicines. When it is necessary to provide medicines, airlines would confirm the reasons for airsickness, and the history of drug allergy, and would ask passengers to fill in "Exemption Form for Passengers to Take Medicine on Board".

For various reasons, passengers may suffer from illness, shock or even death on board. Therefore, the flight attendants shall have enough first-aid knowledge, calmly take effective treatment according to actual conditions of passengers, seek the help of doctors on board when necessary, and get in contact with the ground to arrange the ambulance and medical personnel, and make every effort to protect and save the life of the sick passenger.

晕机是旅客较为常见的不适症状，与晕车、晕船类似。轻者有头晕、胸闷等症状；重者有脸色苍白、呕吐不止、全身冒虚汗等症状。晕机的症状通常在飞机起飞、降落、颠簸、爬升等过程中表现较为明显。乘务员一旦发现旅客有晕机症状，应当主动关心、提供帮助、耐心安抚，并多提供几个清洁袋、热毛巾、温开水等，以舒缓旅客不适症状，帮助其平稳度过乘机时间。

特别注意：航空公司通常不主动提供药品。有必要提供药品时，应当先了解情况，查明晕机原因，询问是否有服用药物过敏史，并要求旅客填写"旅客机上用药免责单"。

由于各种原因，旅客有可能在飞机上出现生病、休克甚至死亡的情况。因此，空乘人员应当掌握必要的急救知识，根据旅客的实际情况沉着应对、有效处理，必要时寻求机上医生的帮助，与地面联络安排救护车和医务人员，尽一切努力保障和挽救旅客的生命。

案例分析

2016年4月24日及25日，南航两个国际航班各有一名旅客在空中突发疾病。南航机组及时启动应急预案，对生病旅客施以救助。两个航班就近备降澳大利亚的机场，为挽救旅客生命赢得了宝贵时间。

问题 并不是每个人都适合乘坐飞机，那么哪些旅客不适宜乘坐飞机？

参考答案

一、心血管疾病患者，特别是心功能不全、心肌缺氧、心肌梗死及严重高血压病人。因空中轻度缺氧，可能使心血管病人旧病复发或病情加重。

二、脑血管病人，如脑栓塞、脑出血、脑肿瘤患者。飞机起降的轰鸣、震动及缺氧等，可使病情加重。

三、呼吸系统疾病患者，如肺气肿、肺心病、气胸。因不适应环境，飞行途中可能因气体膨胀而加重病情。

四、严重贫血者。血红蛋白量水平在50克/升以下者，在飞机上易发生晕厥。

五、耳鼻疾病患者。耳鼻患有急性渗出性炎症，容易导致耳膜穿孔。

六、临近预产期的孕妇，特别是妊娠36周以上的孕妇。空中气压的变化，可能导致胎儿早产。

First Class Service — Scene 06

Situation 22 Prior to Takeoff

任务单

主题：飞机起飞前的头等舱旅客服务。请根据主题和必选项、可选项的要求，编写一段英文对话。

必选项
1. 旅客登机，座位指引
2. 行李服务
3. 自我介绍
4. 告知航班信息（如起飞时间、飞行时长、航路天气等）
5. 易拉得
6. 拖鞋服务
7. 迎宾饮和迎宾毛巾
8. 清理桌面

可选项
1. 头等舱旅客的座位号
2. 旅客携带 / 未携带随身行李
3. 迎宾饮的种类：矿泉水、橙汁、苹果汁等果汁

典型对话

乘务员为头等舱旅客提供引座、行李服务、自我介绍及拖鞋、报纸服务

FA: Good afternoon, Sir. May I have a look at your boarding pass?
先生，下午好！请给我看一下您的登机牌。

P: Yes.
好的。

FA: Mr Zhang, your seat number is B1, just on the left of your hand. May I help you with your bag?

张先生,您的座位在 B1,就在左手边。需要帮您把包放在行李架上吗?

P: Yes, please. Thank you!

好的,谢谢。

FA: Mr. Zhang, may I introduce myself? I am Helen, the cabin manager of this flight. Nice to meet you! It's my pleasure to provide you with cabin service. This is service package for you. There are some newspapers, an eyeshade and so on. These are the slippers. Here you are. Wish you a pleasant journey!

张先生,您好!请允许我自我介绍。我是本次航班乘务长海伦。很高兴见到您。很荣幸为您提供客舱服务。这是为您准备的服务包,里面有报纸、眼罩等。我先帮您把拖鞋打开。祝您旅程愉快!

P: Thanks!

谢谢你!

FA: You are welcome.

不客气。

乘务员为头等舱旅客提供迎宾饮和迎宾毛巾

FA: This is a hot towel for you to wipe your hands, Mr. Zhang. We have prepared mineral water and orange juice for you. Which one do you prefer?

张先生,这是给您的热毛巾,您可以擦一下手。这是为您准备的矿泉水和橙汁,请问您需要哪一种?

P: Mineral water, thank you! By the way, please hang my coat up.

矿泉水吧,谢谢!对了,请帮我挂一下外套。

FA: Yes, do you have any valuables in your coat?

好的,请问您外套里有贵重物品吗?

P: No.

没有。

FA: Mr. Zhang, I have put your coat in the cloakroom. Feel free to let me know when you need it, so that I can bring it for you.

好的,张先生,我帮您把外套挂在衣帽间,有需要我就拿来给您。

P: Thank you!

谢谢!

FA: My pleasure.

很荣幸为您服务。

头等舱旅客饮料饮用完毕，飞机即将起飞

FA： Mr. Zhang, the plane is about to take off. May I clean up the table?

张先生，飞机马上就要起飞了，我帮您整理一下桌面，好吗？

P： Fine.

好的。

FA： Mr. Zhang, may I help you open the window shade, adjust the seat back to the upright position, fasten the seat belt, and stow the tray table? You can adjust the seat back to 180 degrees to make it easy for you to rest when the plane gets into level flight.

张先生，我来帮您打开遮光板、调直座椅靠背、扣好安全带，小桌板帮您收起来。等飞机进入平飞状态，您可以将座椅靠背调整到 180 度，方便您休息。

P： OK.

好的。

高频语句

01 Wish you a pleasant journey!

祝您旅途愉快！

相关表达　Wish you a good journey!

I sincerely hope you have a nice journey!

02 Let me give you a hand.

让我来帮您。

相关表达　Let me help you.

03 May I introduce myself? I am Helen, the cabin manager of this flight.

请允许我自我介绍，我是本次航班的乘务长海伦。

相关表达　I'm your chief flight attendant today.

04 May I help you with your bag?

需要帮您把包放在行李架上吗？

相关表达　Can I put your bag into the baggage compartment overhead?

05 Do you have any valuables in your coat?

您的外套里有贵重物品吗？

相关表达　Could you please check if you have any valuables or documents in your pockets you'd like to keep with you?

Could you remove all valuable items from you pockets?

Are there any valuable items in the pockets that you would like to keep with you?

06 We have a copy of *China Daily, Global Times* and so on.

我们有《中国日报》《环球时报》等报纸。

相关表达　We have *Phoenix Weekly, the CAAC* in-flight magazine and so on.

07 You can adjust the seat back to 180 degrees to make it easy for you to rest when the plane gets into level flight.

等飞机进入平飞状态，您可以把座椅靠背调整180度，方便您休息。

相关表达　You can push the button on the armrest to control you chair.

专业词汇

first class　头等舱　　　　　　　　cloakroom　衣帽间
business class　商务舱　　　　　　　magazine　杂志
economy class/coach　经济舱　　　　chief flight attendant/purser　乘务长

拓展知识

In general, the cabins of a wide-bodied airliner are divided into three classes, namely First Class, Business Class and Ordinary Class (Economy Class). The cabins of a narrow-bodied airliner are divided into two classes, namely, First Class (or Business Class) and Ordinary Class.

At present, the First Class fare for domestic flights is 150% of the full fare of Economy Class, and the Business Class fare is 130% of the full fare of Economy Class.

Both First Class and Business Class provide better environment and service than Economy Class. First Class ranks high, especially. Its outstanding aspects are as below.

• The seats are spacious and comfortable, including standard seats, reclining seats, bed seats and mini suites.

• Supply feather quilt, pajamas, disposable slippers in high quality, personal wash bags, and exclusive lavatories.

• Provides nuts, bread, dessert, dinner, and a wide range of drinks and wines. Besides, meals are served with exquisite tableware, table cloth and napkin.

• Provide a variety of cabin recreations.

通常情况下，宽体客机分为三级客舱结构，即头等舱、商务舱和普通舱（经济舱）；窄体客机分为两级客舱结构，即头等舱（或商务舱）和普通舱。目前，国内航班的头等舱票价为经济舱全票价的150%，商务舱票价为经济舱全票价的130%。头等舱和商务舱的硬件环境和客舱服务标准都比经济舱高，其中，头等舱档次最高。表现为：座椅宽大舒适，有标准座椅、平躺座椅、床式座椅、迷你套房等；提供羽绒被或棉被、睡衣、高质量的一次性拖鞋，个人洗漱包，配有专用盥洗室；提供果仁、面包、甜点、正餐，饮料和酒水品种相对丰富，供餐时使用桌布和餐巾，餐具也颇为考究；提供多样的机舱内娱乐项目。

答疑解惑

对于航空公司来说，根据二八法则，航空公司会想尽法子取悦购买头等舱机票的旅客。

问题 头等舱旅客的要求越来越高。请举例说明各大航空公司对此有何特色服务？

参考答案

达美航空：保时捷接送　　　　马耳他航空：空中 SPA
卡塔尔航空：1000 美元的坐垫　　阿提哈德航空：个人酒吧
新加坡航空：韦奇伍德瓷器餐具（英国顶级瓷器品牌，号称是"世界上最精致的瓷器"）

Situation 23 Cruising

任务单

主题：平飞状态的头等舱旅客服务。请根据主题和必选项、可选项的要求，编写一段英文对话。

必选项
1. 餐前饮
2. 点餐
3. 正餐（热毛巾、示酒、副菜、主菜等）
4. 甜点、水果、面包
5. 餐后饮
6. 征求旅客对菜品的意见
7. 夜航服务

注：饮料和餐食服务过程中，注意铺桌布和提供热毛巾，随时整理桌布

可选项
1. 水果可根据旅客要求在餐前或餐后提供
2. 头等舱饮料种类相较于经济舱更为丰富：苏打水／酒水等
3. 面包的种类：蒜蓉面包、豆沙面包、牛角面包等
4. 主菜、副菜、甜点的种类可自由设定

典型对话

头等舱餐食服务

FA: Mr. Zhang, here is the wine list and menu for you. Please have a look. I'll take your order later.
张先生，您好！这是为您准备的酒水单和餐单，请您过目。稍后我来为您点餐。

P: OK.
好的。

餐前饮服务

FA: Mr. Zhang, what kind of drinks would you like? Orange juice, tomato juice, or soda water?
张先生，您好！您需要点什么饮料呢？橙汁、番茄汁还是苏打水？

P: Soda water.
苏打水。

FA: OK. With ice?
好的，需要加冰吗？

P: No, thank you.

不需要。

FA: Here you are. Enjoy yourself.

您的饮品，请慢用。

点餐

FA: Mr. Zhang, we are going to prepare the dinner for you today. You can choose between kung pao chicken rice and beef noodles with hot green pepper. Both are served with corn and mashed potatoes. Which one do you prefer?

张先生，我们今天为您准备的晚餐，主菜是宫保鸡丁米饭和杭椒牛肉拉面，配菜是玉米粒和土豆泥，请问您需要哪一种？

P: Kung pao chicken rice, please!

宫保鸡丁米饭，谢谢！

FA: OK. Would you like to eat the fruit before or after the meal?

好的，水果先上还是后上呢？

P: Before the meal.

先上吧。

FA: Mr. Zhang, we have some kinds of juice such as orange juice, tomato juice, apple juice and grape juice, and some kinds of soft drinks such as cola, 7-up, coffee and red wine. Which one would you like?

好的，张先生。我们今天为您提供的果汁有橙汁、番茄汁、苹果汁、葡萄汁，软饮料有可乐、七喜，还有咖啡和红酒。请问您需要哪一种？

P: Red wine.

红酒吧。

FA: OK. The red wine for you today is from Australia. I will show it to you later.

好的，今天为您准备的红酒产自澳大利亚，稍后我就为您示酒。

P: All right.

好的。

FA: Mr. Zhang, do you have any special diet?

张先生，您有忌口吗？

P: No.

没有。

FA: Then you have ordered Kung pao chicken rice set meal, served with corn and mashed potatoes, fruit first and red wine. Is that right?

FA: 那我给您重复一下所点的餐食。宫保鸡丁米饭套餐，配菜是玉米粒和土豆泥，水果先上，以及红酒。您看对吗？

P: That's right.

对的。

FA: Please wait a moment. The dinner will be ready in about five minutes.

请稍等。晚餐大约 5 分钟左右备好。

P: Take your time.

好的。

示酒

FA: This is the red wine for you, Mr. Zhang. Please check it.

张先生，这是为您准备的红酒，请您过目。

P: OK. Open it.

好的，打开吧。

铺桌布与餐前毛巾

FA: Mr. Zhang, may I help you with the table cloth?

张先生，我来帮您铺一下桌布，可以吗？

P: Sure.

可以。

FA: A hot towel for you. Do you need any more soda water?

这是为您准备的热毛巾，您的苏打水需要再添加一些吗？

P: No, I don't need any more. Thanks!

不需要了，谢谢！

FA: Shall I take it away?

那我帮您收走，可以吗？

P: Certainly.

好的。

FA: Would you like to try the red wine now?

我现在帮您倒酒，可以吗？

P: Sure.

可以。

FA: This is home cooking series and fruits. Please enjoy your meal.

这是我们航空公司近期推出的家常配菜系列和水果，请慢用。

待旅客副菜用餐完毕

FA: Mr. Zhang, do you mind me making up the table?

张先生，您介意我整理一下您的餐桌吗？

P: No, not at all. Just go head.

当然不，请继续你的工作。

FA: Your main dish, enjoy yourself.

您的主菜，请慢用。

P: Thanks!

谢谢！

待旅客主菜用餐完毕

FA: Mr. Zhang, how do you like the dishes today?

张先生，您觉得今天的菜合您胃口吗？

P: Not bad.

还不错。

FA: May I help you with the table?

我帮您整理一下桌面，可以吗？

P: OK.

好的。

FA: This is the garlic bread and bean paste bread for you today.

这是今天为您提供的蒜蓉面包和豆沙面包，请慢用。

P: No, thank you. I'm fine.

不需要了，谢谢。

FA: OK. The dessert today is cappuccino pyramid. May I bring it to you now?

好的。今天为您提供的甜点是卡布奇诺金字塔，我现在给您拿过来，可以吗？

P: All right.

好的。

提供餐后热饮

FA: Mr. Zhang, would you like some drink after dinner?

张先生，餐后饮品您想喝点什么？

P: Is there hot tea?

有热茶吗？

FA: Of course, there are Tieguanyin, Biluochun and Longjing. Which one do you prefer?

有的。铁观音、碧螺春和龙井，您需要哪种？

P: Tieguanyin tea, please!

铁观音，谢谢！

FA: Please wait a minute.

好的，请稍等。

FA: This is your Tieguanyin tea. Be careful. It is hot.

这是您的铁观音，请小心烫。

P: Thank you!

谢谢！

FA: (After the passenger has finished his tea) May I take the cup away?

（等旅客喝完）我帮您收走，可以吗？

P: Just take it away.

好的。

头等舱乘务员为旅客提供夜航服务

FA: Mr. Zhang, here is a quilt. I'll cover it for you. Now it's 9:30 p.m. It will take us about 6 hours to reach Manhattan as expected.

张先生，您好！这是给您的被子，我帮您盖好。现在时间是夜间9:30，预计还有约6小时到达美国曼哈顿。

P: I see.

好的，谢谢。

FA: You can press the call button at any time if you need any help. Let me help you dim the lights. Have a good rest!

您有需要可以随时叫我，我帮您把灯光调暗，您好好休息！

P: Thanks a lot!

谢谢！

高频语句

01 What would you like for dessert?

您喜欢什么甜点？

相关表达　What would you like best?

　　　　　Which one do you prefer?

02 I'll bring you some snacks / cookies.

我给您拿点小零食 / 饼干过来。

03 May I prepare your table now?

现在可以帮您铺桌布吗?

相关表达　May I lay you the tablecloth for lunch / dinner?

04 May I help you with the table cloth?

我来帮您清理一下桌布可以吗?

相关表达　Do you mind me making up the table?

05 Excuse me, would you want a hot towel?

打扰了,您需要热毛巾吗?

相关表达　This is a hot towel for you.

06 Help yourself.

请慢用。

相关表达　Enjoy yourself, please.

　　　　　I hope you enjoy your drink.

　　　　　Have a good appetite.

07 Let me make the bed for you.

让我来帮您整理床铺吧。

相关表达　Here is a quilt. I'll cover it for you.

　　　　　May I help you make your bed now?

专业词汇

soft drink / alcoholic drink　软饮料 / 酒精饮料

champagne　香槟　　　　　　　　cocktail　鸡尾酒

brandy　白兰地　　　　　　　　　refreshments　茶点

拓展知识

Frequent Flyer Program (FFP) refers to a kind of promotion for customer membership based on miles or points, popular in industries like airline and hotel, to attract more travelers on business and improve the company's competitiveness as well.

As early as the 1980s, airlines began to introduce FFP. In 1994, Air China first introduced FFP and corresponding miles cards (currently named as Phoenix Miles cards) in China. China Eastern Airlines officially launched the FFP in July 1998. Subsequently, Xiamen Airlines, China Southern Airlines and China Northern Airlines also launched their own FFPs.

Airlines have set up clubs to implement the FFP, such as "Air China Club" and "Golden Swallow Club of China Eastern Airlines". Passengers who meet the requirements of airline's FFP may apply to join the club and get a membership card. When passengers book the flight or check in the hotels having partnership with airlines, the miles or points will be credited to their account automatically. Passengers would accordingly earn sufficient miles or points to redeem for a reward ticket or cabin upgrade or other specified rewards.

常旅客计划（Frequent Flyer Program）是指航空公司、酒店等行业向经常使用其产品的客户推出的以里程累积或积分累积获得奖励的促销手段，是一种吸引商务旅客、提高公司竞争力的市场手段。

早在20世纪80年代初，航空公司就开始引入常旅客计划。1994年，中国国际航空公司在国内最早推出了常旅客计划和相应的知音卡（现名为凤凰知音卡）。中国东方航空公司1998年7月正式推出了常旅客计划。随后，厦航、南航、北航等也相继推出了自己的常旅客计划。

航空公司为实施常旅客计划，均成立了俱乐部，如"国航俱乐部""东航金燕俱乐部"等。符合各航空公司常旅客计划要求的旅客均可申请加入相应航空公司的俱乐部，并得到一张会员卡。会员通过乘坐该航空公司的航班而得到里程，也可通过在该航空公司的合作伙伴，如酒店处消费而得到里程。当里程达到一定标准时，会员可用所得里程换取免费机票、免费升舱或其他指定的奖励。

案例分析

云端之上喝酒是一种怎样的感觉？很多航空公司的商务舱和头等舱都会提供丰富酒品，令旅客体验飞机上曼妙的杯酒人生。

旅客小鹏第一次坐法航的商务舱时，看到酒单上20多种红葡萄酒、白葡萄酒、香槟以及威士忌，一时不知如何选择。法航荷航大中国区公关部经理周英慧说，其实那些深谙美酒文化的旅客，可以很容易从繁复的酒单中选到符合自己口味的那一款。不过，小鹏这样的旅客也不必过于纠结，因为法航机舱内设有专业配酒师，专门为旅客用餐配酒提供服务，整个航程中只在用餐时出现。

商旅常客 David 印象最深刻的是阿联酋航空空客 A380 头等舱的酒吧。"包厢就像酒店客房，有时候可以到大堂的酒吧里坐坐，喝上一杯，聊聊天。"这里提供数十种酒品，包括 1996 年的 Chateau Lynch Bages（靓次伯红酒）、2001 年的 Nuits St Georges 1er Cru Aux Perdrix（勃艮第红酒），以及法国白葡萄酒、澳洲红酒、调酒师现场调制的鸡尾酒等。其中最奢华的一款当属 Cuvee Dom Perignon（法国唐培里侬香槟），"要知道，曾经一款 1990 年的拍到了 1035 美元。"除了美酒，机上酒吧还是非常奇妙的社交场所，比如你能遇到一位潜在的生意伙伴，或一位风趣的朋友。

周英慧说，在飞机上点酒也颇有讲究，"可以先选择一杯香槟作为开胃酒，舒缓精神；用餐时根据菜品和喜好，选择红葡萄酒或白葡萄酒；餐后可以再来点消化酒，比如干邑，而且有助于睡眠。"

曾有一位女旅客乘坐加拿大航空经济舱，一口气品尝了几种红酒。当空姐得知她是一位美食家时，特别为她取了一杯头等舱的白葡萄酒。

问题 飞机上提供酒水服务，有什么需要特别注意的？

参考答案

单宁不宜过重

同样一瓶葡萄酒，在地上和万米高空饮用，口感会有所不同。由于高空中机舱增压、空气干燥，人们通常会失去 1/3 的嗅觉，味蕾也会扭曲酒体。对于葡萄酒来说，酸度和单宁会被强化，糖分和酒精的感觉则会减弱。因此地面上的好酒，在空中不一定是好酒，那些酸度过高、单宁过重的葡萄酒就不太适合。根据这些条件，通常航空公司的品酒师会在制订酒单时为客人做精心选择，因此酒单上的酒品都是适合空中饮用的。

新酒换旧酒

飞机上为了减少沉淀物的出现，会把需要换瓶的陈年酒酿排除在外，全部选择满瓶装的新酒，以保证最佳的品酒体验。

Situation 24 Prior to Landing

任务单

主题：头等舱旅客下机前的服务。请根据主题和必选项、可选项的要求，编写一段英文对话。

必选项
1. 热毛巾
2. 征求旅客意见（填写航空公司服务反馈表）
3. 回收服务反馈表、iPad、被子等
4. 告知其具体的落地时间
5. 外套服务
6. 美好祝愿

可选项
1. 旅客满意 / 不太满意
2. 目的地地面温度较高 / 较低
3. 下机通过廊桥 / 摆渡车

典型对话

头等舱乘务员征求旅客的意见

FA: Mr. Zhang, what do you think of our cabin service during the flight?
张先生，在本次航班的服务过程中，您觉得我们的服务怎么样？

P: Very good!
非常好！

FA: Thank you for your praise! Would you please give us some valuable suggestions?
谢谢您的肯定！请您留下宝贵建议。

落地前 30 分钟

FA: Mr. Zhang, we will be landing in a short while. Can I take these away (service feedback forms, the iPad and quilts provided by the airline)?
张先生，飞机马上就要降落了。我收走这些(服务反馈表、航空公司提供的iPad和被子等)可以吗？

P: OK.
好的。

FA: Mr. Zhang, I am very glad to have spent some precious time with you. Thank you very much for your valuable advice. You will arrive Manhattan in about 5 minutes. The ground temperature is 20 degrees Celsius. You might feel a little bit cool. How about bringing your heavy coat right away?

张先生，很高兴与您共同度过了一段宝贵时光，也非常感谢您提出的宝贵建议。约5分钟后您会到达曼哈顿。当地地面温度是20摄氏度，可能会有点凉爽，您的厚外套我现在给您拿过来可以吗？

P: OK. Thanks!

好的，谢谢！

FA: This is your coat, Mr. Zhang. We will dock at the boarding later, and you might have to remain seated and wait for several minutes. I'll let you know in time after the connection. Is that OK?

张先生，这是您的外套。稍后我们会对接廊桥，您需要在座位上等待一段时间。对接好之后我会及时告知您，可以吗？

P: Sure.

可以。

高频语句

01 What do you think of our cabin service during the flight?
在本次航班的服务过程中，您觉得我们的服务怎么样？

02 Would you please give us some valuable suggestions?
请您留下宝贵建议。

03 I am very glad to have spent some precious time with you, and thank you very much for your valuable advice.
很高兴与您共同度过了一段宝贵时光，也非常感谢您提出的宝贵建议。

04 Thank you for your support to our company for such a long time.
感谢您长期以来对我们公司的支持。

05 The ground temperature is 20 degrees Celsius. You might feel a little bit cool.
地面温度是20摄氏度，可能会有点凉爽。
相关表达　It is a little bit windy.

06 We will dock at the boarding later, and you might have to remain seated and wait for several minutes.
稍后我们会对接廊桥，您需要在座位上等待一段时间。

相关表达　Please wait here for a while until the boarding bridge is in position.

　　　　　　Please take the transit bus after landing.

专业词汇

dock　停靠、进港

feedback form　（航空公司服务）反馈表

connection　对接

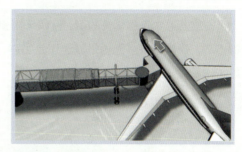

bridge　廊桥

拓展知识

Time zone is a region of the globe that observes a uniform standard time. 24 time zones came into being in the international longitude conference held in Washington in 1884, so as to overcome the confusion of time.

The international conference decided to divide the earth's surface into one-by-one zones from east to west along the longitude, and specified that the time in two adjacent zones is one hour apart. People in the eastern and western parts of the same zone see the sun rise at most one hour apart. When people cross a zone, they may adjust their clocks by one hour (to reduce one hour when westward, and add one hour when eastward). If they cross more than one zone, they may add or reduce a few hours corresponding to the number of the zones across, which makes it very convenient to tell the time.

Today the world is divided into 24 time zones. And the line of langitude which passed through the Royal Observatory Green wich near London, UK is defined as the prime meridian, namely zero longitude. China takes the time of UTC +8:00 in Beijing as the unified time nationwide.

时区（time zone）是指地球上的区域使用同一个时间定义。1884年在华盛顿召开国际经度会议时，为了克服时间上的混乱，规定将全球划分为24个时区。有关国际会议决定将地球表面按经线从东到西，划成一个个区域，并且规定相邻区域的时间相差1小时。在同一区域内的东端和西端的人看到太阳升起的时间最多相差不过1小时。当人们跨过一个区域，就将自己的时钟校正1小时（向西减1小时，向东加1小时），跨过几个区域就加减几小时。这样计算时间就很方便。现今全球共分为 24 个时区,并且规定通过英国伦敦格林尼治古天文台的那条经线称为本初子午线,即零度经线。在中国采用首都北京所在地东八区的时间为全国统一使用时间。

答疑解惑

出国旅游原本是件愉快的事,但如果搭长途飞机远游,有些人可能会因为时差问题而失眠、精神不济,影响游兴。无论是旅游还是出差,尽快调整生理时钟适应当地作息时间,可提高旅行或工作质量。

应如何做来减少时差的影响?

参考答案

出发前

一、预先随时区变化调整作息。出发前数日,配合即将前往的时区,调整睡眠时间,帮助身体适应新时区。每次调整 30~60 分钟,逐日增加。这样做可使身体不必那么突然或费力地适应新时区。

二、尽量安排夜间飞行,这是复制正常作息的上策。

三、提早打包行李,以避免出发临近压力和焦虑。

飞行中

四、适足摄取水分。水是减少时差的利器,少碰酒精和含咖啡因的饮品。

五、保持血液流通。坐得越久,越易昏睡。运动也是反时差利器,飞机处于平飞状态时,可以定时起身,在过道上踱步,伸展肢体。这些方法有助于加强血液流通,血流通畅则身心舒活、有元气。

六、自然光。抵达目的地后接触自然日光,有助于加快重设生物钟。

抵达后

七、就寝时间以前别睡。尽量维持正常睡眠量,避免打乱在新时区的固定睡眠。除非在接近就寝时间之际抵达,否则应保持清醒,忍住小睡的诱惑。

Scene 07

Dealing with Different Situations

Situation 25 Delay

任务单

主题：旅客已经登机，飞机因为某种原因延误，无法按时起飞。请根据主题和必选项、可选项的要求，编写一段延误广播。

必选项
1. 非常抱歉地通知旅客飞机延误
2. 告知旅客延误原因
3. 告知旅客预计起飞时间
4. 告知旅客延误期间的特殊服务或处理方案

可选项
1. 延误原因：天气／空中交通管制／飞机机械故障／飞机需要除冰／跑道需要除冰／货物超重／行李装载原因／临时增加餐食／旅客乘机手续尚未办妥／旅客临时取消行程，地勤正在查找其行李／航路上有军事禁令
2. 预计起飞时间：20分钟后／1小时后
3. 等待期间为旅客提供饮料／餐食／报纸／录像

典型对话

延误广播：航班因空中交通管制原因延误，预计起飞时间为大约2小时后，等待期间为旅客提供饮料服务

Ladies and gentlemen, may I have your attention please? Our departure will be delayed for about two hours, as we are waiting for air traffic control clearance. Please remain seated and refrain from smoking. In the meantime, we will offer beverages. On behalf of Air China, we apologize for any inconvenience caused and thank you for your patience and kind understanding!

女士们、先生们，很抱歉地通知您，由于机场交通管制，我们的飞机暂时不能起飞，预计大约 2 小时后起飞。请您在座位上耐心等候。本航班为禁烟航班。稍后，客舱乘务员将为您提供饮料服务。给您造成的不便，我们深表歉意。谨代表国航感谢您的理解与配合！

等待广播：因机场繁忙，飞机正在跑道上等待起飞命令，约 10 分钟后起飞

Ladies and gentlemen, may I have your attention please? We are sorry to inform you that we will take off in about 10 minutes, as we are waiting air traffic control clearance. Please remain seated and refrain from smoking. Thank you!

女士们、先生们，请注意。由于机场繁忙，我们正在等待起飞命令，飞机大约在 10 分钟后起飞。请您在原座休息等待，请不要吸烟。谢谢！

等待广播：因部分旅客尚未办理完登机手续，地勤人员正在积极协助办理，需要等待

Ladies and gentlemen, we are waiting for some passengers to complete the boarding procedures. Our ground staff has advised us that these passengers will join us as soon as possible. Thank you!

女士们、先生们，由于部分旅客还没有办完登机手续，地面工作人员正在积极协助办理中。请稍候，谢谢！

下飞机等待广播：因天气原因需要等待较长时间，因此安排旅客到候机厅休息等候

Ladies and gentlemen, the captain has informed us that our flight will be delayed because of bad weather conditions. We ask that you wait in the terminal. Please take your ticket and boarding pass, and disembark. Your carry-on items may be left on board, but be sure to carry the valuables. Our ground staff will announce the latest information in the broadcast. We apologize for the inconvenience caused. Thank you for your understanding and cooperation！

女士们、先生们，接到机长通知，由于天气恶劣，飞机暂时不能起飞。我们将安排您到候机厅休息等候。请配合我们的工作，带好您的机票、登机牌下飞机。您的随身行李可以放在飞机上，但贵重物品请随身携带。如有进一步的消息，地面人员将随时广播通知您。由此给您带来的不便，我们深表歉意。感谢您的理解和配合！

旅客未听清广播内容，询问延误情况

P：Excuse me, what is going on?
　　你好，发生什么事了？

FA: We will wait until a takeoff clearance is given, owing to the air traffic control.

由于交通管制,我们的飞机需等待起飞指令。

P: When shall we take off? I have a very important meeting at 2:00 p.m.

那飞机什么时候可以起飞呢?我下午两点有个很重要的会议。

FA: Our departure will be delayed for about half an hour. The delay shouldn't be too long.

预计起飞时间是约 30 分钟后,应该不会延误太久。

P: I certainly hope so.

但愿如此。

高频语句

01　The flight has been delayed because of bad weather.

由于天气恶劣,航班延误。

相关表达　The flight has been delayed due to some mechanical troubles.

The flight will be delayed for 2 hours owing to ground heavy fog.

02　The engineers are making a careful examination over the plane.

机务维修人员正在仔细检查飞机。

03　The airport of our destination has been closed. The reason is unknown at the moment.

目的地机场已关闭,原因尚不清楚。

04　We'll be leaving as soon as we receive takeoff clearance.

我们一旦得到放飞许可,就能起飞离开。

相关表达　We will be leaving as soon as the weather gets better.

The plane will take off as soon as a clearance is given.

05　We have to divert to Guangzhou airport due to heavy rain in the Shenzhen area.

由于深圳地区大雨,我们不得不改飞广州机场。

06　We have just been informed that this flight has been cancelled.

我们接到通知,本次航班取消。

07　We'll have to stay here overnight. Please take your belongings and prepare to disembark. Your accommodation will be arranged by our airline.

我们将在这里过夜,请拿好随身物品准备下飞机。您的食宿将由我们航空公司负责。

相关表达　We will provide free accommodation for every passenger.

08 If we have any further information, we'll let you know immediately.

如有进一步的消息，我们会立即通知大家。

专业词汇

weather office　气象站　　　　　　　　bad weather　恶劣天气
heavy rain/thunderstorm　大雨、雷暴雨　lightning　闪电
snow storm　暴风雪　　　　　　　　　　ground heavy fog　（机场）地面大雾
mechanical troubles　机械故障

拓展知识

Flight delays have become one of the most prominent problems affecting the quality of aviation services. There are many factors causing flight delays, such as bad weather, air traffic control, passengers, airlines or airports. For the specific reasons, it may be that the weather on the airports during takeoff and landing and even on the route is bad, or that the radio interferes with the normal operation of the aircraft, or that the advertising balloons lift off illegally, or that residents around the airport fly kites, or that pigeons and migrant birds fly over, or that there are military injunctions on the route, or that a passenger's check-in procedure has not yet been completed, or that passengers who have checked in and cancelled their journey, or that there is baggage overloading or baggage loading, or that there is temporary increase in meals, or aircraft mechanical failure, or that the airplane needs deicing, or that the runway needs deicing.

航班延误目前已经成为影响航空服务质量最为突出的问题之一。导致航班延误的原因是多方面的，通常包括恶劣天气、空中交通管制、旅客原因以及航空公司和机场原因等。具体原因包括起降机场甚至航路上天气原因、无线电干扰飞机正常运行、广告气球非法升空、机场周边居民放风筝、鸽子或候鸟飞过、航路上有军事禁令、旅客乘机手续尚未办妥、旅客已办理登机

手续又临时取消行程、货物超重、行李装载、临时增加餐食、飞机机械故障、飞机需要除冰、跑道需要除冰等。

案例分析

2017年9月10日,一架原定当晚21:15从成都双流机场起飞前往美国洛杉矶的海航HU469航班延误了15个小时。其间有旅客反映,一位戴着海航标志牌的工作人员告诉旅客,是"机长拿错护照导致飞机延误"。事后海航工作人员表示,该航班延误是由于"公司原因",海航已做出赔偿。

问题 航班延误一定会得到赔偿吗?

中国民航总局于2016年7月出台《国内航空公司因自身原因造成航班延误给予旅客经济补偿》的政策(以下简称为《延误补偿》),确保旅客在航班延误情况发生后能够拿到补偿。《延误补偿》要求,航空公司因自身原因造成的航班延误必须给予旅客补偿。其中,航班延误时段分4小时~8小时、8小时以上两种,补偿标准在100元~200元,各个航空公司可根据自身经济实力确定具体的补偿标准。由境外回国的航班延误补偿标准,可以参照当地的法规。

需要注意的是,不是航班延误了航空公司就一定要赔偿,具体还要区分航班延误原因以及是否给旅客直接造成可预见性损失。如果因为航空公司的主观原因,如一般的"技术性问题"导致航班延误,旅客可以要求赔偿;如果因为天气等非主观原因导致航班延误,航空公司可以不赔偿。目前不少保险公司推出了"航班延误险"供旅客选择购买。

Situation 26 Complaints

任务单

主题：乘务员处理旅客抱怨。请根据主题和必选项、可选项的要求编写一段英文对话。

必选项
1. 主动解答旅客的疑问或抱怨。
2. 主动致歉。
3. 安抚旅客情绪。
4. 在力所能及的范围内解答或解决旅客的问题。

可选项
抱怨原因：
1. 旅客因航班延误产生抱怨。
2. 旅客因行李摆放问题产生抱怨。
3. 旅客因餐食问题产生抱怨。
4. 旅客因座位问题产生抱怨。
5. 旅客与周边旅客发生冲突。

典型对话

航班延误，旅客等待时间较长向乘务员抱怨

P: Excuse me, the plane over there is about to take off. Why are we still here?
为什么那架飞机都可以起飞了，我们怎么还在等待？

FA: I'm very sorry. But we are still waiting for clearance from the air traffic control tower.
非常抱歉。我们的航班由于交通管制的原因暂时还没有得到起飞的指令。

P: Oh! my god. I am going to have business talk with important customers. I can't afford being late for that.
噢，天啊！我要跟非常重要的顾客谈生意，实在不能迟到啊。

FA: I understand your feeling. We didn't expect to delay, either.
我能理解您的心情。我们都不期望延误。

P: Alright. Tell me how long shall I wait at most?
好吧，那你说我最多要在这儿等多久。

FA: I am not very clear, Sir. But we will take off once receiving departure clearance from the air traffic control tower.
这很难说。不过，航路管制一经解除，我们即刻起飞。

P: Then I'd like to be informed if we are going to take off.

好吧，一旦放飞，你告诉我一下。

FA: No problem. Shall I bring you a cup of water?

当然可以。需要我给您拿杯水吗？

P: Yes, thank you!

好的，谢谢！

配餐主食只余 1 种，旅客想要的没有了，向乘务员抱怨

FA: Dear Sir, here's the meal.

先生，您好。这是为您准备的餐食。

P: Chicken rice, please.

鸡肉米饭。谢谢。

FA: Sorry. No chicken rice now. How about beef noodles?

抱歉，鸡肉米饭没有了。主食只有牛肉面条了。您看行不行？

P: I do prefer chicken rice.

我就爱吃鸡肉米饭。

FA: Well, I'll check for you. A second.

我再去服务间帮您看一下。请稍等。

P: OK.

好的。

（FA goes towards the kitchen and is back a few minutes later.）

FA: Pitifully, we don't have any chicken rice. How about trying beef noodles? It's tasty too.

真遗憾，鸡肉米饭没有了。牛肉面条也很好，您试试？

P: All right.

好吧。

小孩哭闹，周边旅客不满，向乘务员抱怨

P: Excuse me, Miss.

您好，女士。

FA: Yes. Is there anything I can do for you?

先生，您好。有什么可以帮您的？

P: The baby over there is crying too loudly. It's a bit annoying.

那边的小孩哭闹声挺大，有些烦。

FA: Sorry for the inconvenience for you. I'll go and check.

给您带来不便，非常抱歉。我去看一看。

(FA goes towards the passenger with the infant.)

FA: Hello, the baby is crying. Would you like some assistance?

宝宝真可爱，怎么哭了呢？需要帮忙吗？

P: Sorry for the noise. She's hungry, I think.

抱歉打搅大家。她可能饿了。

FA: May I help you with the powdered milk?

需要我帮忙冲泡奶粉吗？

P: Sure. Thank you.

好的，非常感谢。

FA: My pleasure.

不客气。

(FA goes towards the passenger who complains.)

FA: Excuse me. The baby was hungry and cried a bit. It's OK now. Thank you for your understanding and patience.

抱歉，刚才小朋友肚子饿了，有些哭闹，现在已经安抚好了。感谢您的理解与耐心。

P: OK. Thank you.

好的，谢谢。

高频语句

01 I do apologize.

实在抱歉。

相关表达　I'm sorry.

Please accept my apology.

02 Would you please put your bag into the overhead compartment?

您能将行李包放在头顶上方的行李架上吗？

相关表达　For your safety, would you mind putting it into the overhead compartment?

03 How about placing it under the seat in front you?

将它放在您前面座位底下可以吗？

相关表达　You may put it under the seat in front of you.

④ Please put the baggage in the overhead compartment or under the seat in front of you to keep the aisle clear.

为了保持客舱通道畅通，请您将行李放在行李架上或座椅前方的挡杆区域内。

相关表达　For the safety of you and other passengers, the luggage needs to be put in rows.

I'm afraid you could not put your suitcase on the empty seat.

No luggage in anywhere of the emergency exit area to keep the passage clear.

⑤ Passengers are not allowed to change seats, according to the epidemic prevention and control requirements.

根据疫情防控的要求，客舱内不允许调换座位。

相关表达　Better not to change the seats for the health and safety of both of you.

⑥ I can understand your feeling. I will do my best.

我能理解您的感受，我一定尽力帮助您。

相关表达　We will try our best to help you.

I can fully understand you.

专业词汇

apologize　抱歉　　　　　　　　departure/ arrival time　起飞 / 到达时间
claims/indemnity　索赔　　　　　penalty　罚款

拓展知识

During the process of cabin service, flight delays, conflicts with nearby passengers, discontent on the provided products or service may lead to dissatisfaction or even complaints from passengers. In such cases, the flight attendants should respect passengers, think about from the passengers' position, seek for understanding and try the best to solve problems. Only with these concepts could the flight attendants properly deal with passengers' complaints by asking and replying patiently, analyzing where goes wrong, making a sound judgment, sincerely apologizing, comforting passengers, solving the problem within their power and keeping records accordingly.

在客舱服务过程中，由于延误、与周边旅客冲突、提供产品或服务不周到等一些原因，可能引起旅客的不满甚至是投诉。遇到此类事情，乘务员应当秉承以客为尊、换位思考、寻求理解、尽力解决的理念，妥善处理旅客抱怨，耐心询问答疑，分析判断问题根源，合理判断，诚挚致歉，安抚好旅客，在力所能及的范围内解决处理，并做好相关记录。

案例分析

12B 座陈女士一入座便要求更换座位，而且必须是两个相邻的座位，因为是两人同行。换座起因是陈女士嫌弃 12C 座的旅客一身酒气，又不好意思当面说。但整个客舱找遍了只有最后一排的两个相邻座位是空位，而陈女士坚决不同意去最后一排就座，认为是 12C 座影响了她，应该把 12C 换走。12C 的旅客大发雷霆，与陈女士发生了口角。

问题 面对机上的纠纷与旅客的抱怨，乘务员应如何处理？

参考答案

乘务员倒来茶水安抚满身酒气的 12C 旅客；即刻再次为陈女士寻找靠前的相邻的空座，无果后再次向其致歉。于是陈女士提出升至头等舱，可当时头等舱的座位情况也无法实现两个相邻空座的要求，而且打扰头等舱旅客实属不妥。但陈女士不听劝说，坚持要升舱，乘务员又从头等舱富余的餐食中取了一份给陈女士，并说："现在头等舱的旅客都已经休息了，不便再去打搅大家。很抱歉我们的服务没能达到您的要求。这是为您准备的头等舱餐食。您虽然无法升至头等舱，但我们会尽最大的努力为您提供头等舱般的服务，也希望您能支持我们的工作。"待陈女士用餐结束后，乘务员又为她和她的同行朋友取来头等舱富余的水果，陈女士情绪好转，向乘务员表示感谢。

地面工作人员与空中工作人员因迎客时未能有效发现带有酒气的旅客，可能导致其他旅客的不愉快反应。面对机上的纠纷与旅客的抱怨，在允许的范围内，乘务员要善用机上资源，高效真诚地沟通，尽力安抚旅客情绪、解决问题。

Situation 27 Emergency

任务单

主题：客舱内发生紧急情况，需要进行客舱广播。请根据主题和必选项、可选项的要求，编写一段英文广播词。

必选项	以乘务长/乘务员的身份进行紧急情况客舱广播（不包含机长广播部分内容）
可选项	紧急情况： 1. 客舱起火/客舱灭火后 2. 客舱释压/紧急失密/飞机到达安全高度后 3. 陆地或水上迫降/最后确认/飞机紧急着陆或触水前/飞机紧急着陆或触水后广播 4. 出口说明/防冲击姿势/取下尖锐物品/客舱行李安排

典型对话

颠簸广播

Ladies and gentlemen, our aircraft is experiencing some turbulence. Please return to your seat and fasten your seat belt. Please don't use the lavatories. Cabin service will be suspended during this period. We apologize for any inconvenience caused. Thank you for your cooperation!

女士们、先生们，受航路气流的影响，我们的飞机遇有颠簸。请您回原位坐好，系好安全带。颠簸期间，洗手间暂停使用。同时，我们将暂停客舱服务，带来不便，敬请谅解。谢谢您的合作！

客舱失火广播

Ladies and gentlemen, a minor fire broke out in the rear cabin. We are quickly controlling the situation. We require all passengers to remain seated and keep calm and follow the instructions of the crew. Affected passengers are requested to change your seats. Smoking is not allowed. Thank you!

女士们、先生们，现在客舱后部有一处失火。我们正在组织灭火。请大家原位坐好不要惊慌，听从乘务员的指挥。我们将调整火源附近旅客的座位，其他旅客请不要在客舱内走动。严禁吸烟。谢谢！

客舱释压广播

Ladies and gentlemen, our plane is now experiencing decompression. Oxygen masks have dropped automatically from the overhead compartment above your seats. Fasten your seat belt; pull a mask sharply toward you and place the mask over your nose and mouth. Pull the elastic band over your head. Remain calm and breathe normally. If you are traveling with a child, attend to yourself first and then the child. Smoking is not allowed.

女士们、先生们，现在发生客舱释压。您座椅上方行李架内的氧气面罩已自动脱落。请系好安全带。用力拉下氧气面罩，并将面罩罩在口鼻处，带子套在头上。请保持镇静，进行正常呼吸。如果您与儿童相邻而坐，请先戴好自己的面罩，再帮儿童戴上面罩。严禁吸烟。

陆地／水上迫降广播

Ladies and gentlemen, your attention please. This is your cabin manager. It is necessary for us to make an emergency landing/ditching. The crew are well trained to handle this type of situation. Please return to your seats, keep calm and follow the instructions of the crew. Put your seat backs to the upright position and stow all tray tables. Put all of your baggage under the seat in front of you or in the overhead compartment.

女士们、先生们，请注意。我是本次航班的乘务长。本架飞机须陆地／水上紧急迫降，我们全体机组成员都受过良好的训练，以应对此类紧急情况。现在请您回到原位，保持镇静，听从乘务员的指挥。请调直座椅靠背，收起小桌板。请把所有的行李放在前面座椅下方或行李箱内。

防冲击姿势广播

Ladies and gentlemen, the crew will now explain the brace position to you. The brace command is "HEADS DOWN, BRACE". When you hear "BRACE FOR IMPACT", put your legs apart, place your feet flat on the floor. Cross your arms like this. Lean forward as far as possible, and hold the seat back in front of you, rest your face on your arms. Remain this position until you hear the command "UNFASTEN SEATBELTS". Be careful that there are multiple impact senses before the plane stops completely.

女士们、先生们，现在乘务员向您介绍防冲击姿势。口令是"低头、抱紧。"当您听到"抱紧、防撞"的口令时，两腿分开，两脚平放在地。双臂如此交叉，尽量向前倾，抓住前方座椅椅背，头放在两臂之间，保持防冲击姿势直到听到"解开安全带"的口令。请注意，在飞机完全停稳前，会有多次撞击感。

取下尖锐物品和客舱行李安排

Ladies and gentlemen, please remove all sharp objects, such as eyeglasses, dentures, pens, watches and jewelry. Remove your neckties and scarves. Put these items in your hand luggage. Do not put anything in the seat-pocket in front of you. Remove your shoes and hand them to the crew. Thank you!

女士们、先生们，现在请取下随身的尖锐物品，如眼镜、假牙、钢笔、手表和首饰，解开领带和围巾。把所有这些物品放入行李内，请不要把任何东西放在您前面的座椅口袋内。请脱下鞋子交由乘务员保管。谢谢！

旅客发现有失火燃烧的味道

FA： Hello, Lady. What can I do for you?
　　 您好，女士。有什么可以帮您的？
P： Yes, I just smelled a smell of burning. What's wrong?
　　 我刚刚闻到有烧焦的味道。发生什么事了？
FA： Don't worry. A minor fire broke out in the lavatory of rear cabin.
　　 别担心，客舱后部的洗手间有一小处失火。
P： I am sacred about it.
　　 好可怕。
FA： Just take it easy. It is under control.
　　 别担心，已经完全控制住了。
P： OK.
　　 好吧。

高频语句

01　All the passengers must be evacuated.
　　 必须撤离所有的旅客。

(02) Oxygen masks have dropped from the overhead compartment above your seats.

您座椅上方行李架内的氧气面罩已掉落。

相关表达　Oxygen masks will drop down from the compartment above your head if there is any change in the cabin pressure.

　　　　　The oxygen masks are in panel over your head.

(03) If you are traveling with a child, attend to yourself first and then the child.

如果您与儿童同行，请先佩戴好您的面罩，然后再为儿童佩戴。

相关表达　If you have an infant with you, please put on the oxygen mask first, and then the infant.

(04) Life vest is under your seat.

救生衣在您座椅的下方。

相关表达　You may take your life vest from the underside of your seat.

(05) Please locate the emergency exit nearest to you.

请找准离您最近的紧急出口。

(06) Ladies and gentlemen, please remove all sharp objects, such as eyeglasses, dentures, pens, watches and jewelry. Please remove your neckties and scarves.

女士们、先生们，请取下所有的尖锐物品，如眼镜、假牙、钢笔、手表、首饰等。请取下您的领带和围巾。

(07) We are now passing through the turbulence.

我们正遇到颠簸。

相关表达　We are now encountering some turbulence.

　　　　　Lavatories can't be used because of turbulence.

(08) Brace for impact according to my instruction.

请根据我的口令做好防冲击姿势。

专业词汇

turbulence　颠簸　　　　　　　extinguisher　灭火器
escape rope　紧急用绳　　　　 emergency landing / ditching　陆上 / 水上紧急迫降

拓展知识

　　Forced landing refers to a conscious emergency landing on the ground or on the water at or outside the airport since the airplane cannot continue the flight due to unexpected circumstances. Forced landing has high requirements for the landing position and aircraft performance, so there are high risks that it may lead to a fatal crash. Unexpected circumstances that may lead to forced landing include the failure of mechanical, hydraulic, or electrical equipment of an aircraft (e.g. The landing gear cannot be extended normally), fire, collision with other aircrafts or objects in the air, the life in danger in terms of crew or passengers in injury or illness, the aircraft disorientation or fuel exteustion, suddenly bad weather, hijacking or illegal crossings, or disobedience of the air traffic control.

In case of these accidents, the pilot should use the equipment to detect or determine the seriousness of the problem and take appropriate measures in a timely manner to minimize the potential danger. Fire fighting measures should be taken as soon as possible in case of fire. On a multi-engined aircraft, if the engine stops runnings, the pilot should adjust the rest engines properly, as well as properly step on the pedals to correct the aileron, and offset the unbalanced thrust, so as to maintain normal flight conditions. On a single-engined plane, if the engine stops running and cannot restart, is ineffective, the pilot can only glide to the right place to land.

Forced landing is generally divided into land forced landing, which refers to landing on the ground, and ditching, which refers to landing on the ocean, lake or other waters. Ditching requires the water to the land as close as possible, and is more dangerous than land forced landing. When the aircraft lands at the airport, if the landing gear can not be automatically extended, it shall be put down through manual control. If the manual control is invalid, the aircraft should be landed on its belly.

迫降（forced landing）指飞机因意外情况不能继续飞行而在机场或机场以外的地面或水面上进行的有意识紧急降落。因迫降对落点环境及飞行器的性能要求很高，所以存在着较大风险，常有可能机毁人亡。导致迫降的意外情况有：飞机的机械、液压或电气设备失灵（如起落架无法正常展开），火灾，在空中与别的飞机或物体相撞，机上人员伤病、有生命危险，飞机迷航燃料用尽，天气条件突然变坏，劫机或非法越境，不服从空中交通管制等。

发生这些意外情况时，飞行员应利用机上设备进行检测或判断，确定问题的严重程度，及时采取适当措施使潜在危险减至最低程度。发生火灾时，应立即按规定采取灭火措施。在多发动机飞机上,若一台发动机停止工作,应适当调节其余发动机,轻踩脚蹬校正副翼,抵消不平衡的推力,以便保持正常的飞行状态。在单发动机飞机上,若发动机停止工作且空中起动无效,就只能滑翔到适当的地方着陆。

迫降一般分为陆上迫降和水上迫降。陆上迫降指着陆场地在陆地;水上迫降指着陆场地在海洋、湖泊等水面上。水上迫降要求尽可能靠近陆地,水上迫降危险性高于陆上迫降。在机场内着陆时,若起落架不能自动放下,则用手控放下;如手动无效,则用机腹擦地着陆。

案例分析

2017年9月5日,一架从日本羽田机场出发前往纽约的日本航空客机因机体故障被迫返航,在机场紧急着陆,所幸无人员伤亡。

问题 陆上迫降和水上迫降的紧急撤离时间分别是多少秒?

参考答案

陆上迫降的紧急撤离时间为90秒,水上迫降的紧急撤离时间为120秒。

Situation 28 Suspected Infectious Diseases

任务单

主题：航班上，忽然发现旅客有疑似传染病症状。请根据主题和必选项、可选项的要求编写一段英文对话。

必选项	1. 及时发现旅客身体不舒服，并主动关心。 2. 发现旅客有疑似传染病症状，及时报告乘务长。 3. 乘务员到服务舱拿应急医疗箱和卫生防疫包，做好个人防护后妥善处置。 4. 为疑似传染病旅客及周边旅客提供必要个人防护用品。 5. 收集疑似传染病旅客及周边旅客的个人信息。
可选项	1. 旅客症状：非常明显不适 / 持续性干咳 / 呼吸困难 / 持续性腹泻 / 持续性呕吐 / 身体皮肤出现红疹 / 不明原因的淤青和流血 / 与确诊的传染病人有密切接触史。 2. 相关工作可由多名乘务员配合完成。

典型对话

乘务员发现旅客咳嗽不止，主动关心

FA: Are you OK, Sir?
您还好吗，先生？

P: I have a skin rash, feel cold, and cough a lot. I've vomited several times, too.
我皮肤出现红疹、浑身发凉、咳嗽，刚刚还呕吐了几次。

FA: Well, don't worry. We will stay with you and I will inform my manager.
别担心，我们会一直陪着您，同时我将报告我们乘务长。

乘务员通过内话系统报告乘务长

FA: Purser, there is a medical case. The passenger seated in 48C has symptoms of a skin rash, persistent coughing and vomiting. He is appearing obviously unwell.
报告乘务长，有情况。48C 旅客皮疹、咳嗽不止、呕吐，感觉很不舒服。

P: Copy that. Please carry on the universal precautions procedure and pay close attention to the passenger. I'll report to Captain immediately.
收到，请立即做好个人防护，密切关注旅客。我来报告机长。

FA: Get it.

好的。

（做好个人防护后）乘务员为旅客测量体温并安置旅客

FA: Dear Sir, may I take your temperature, please?

先生，给您量一下体温。

（体温计显示温度 38.5 摄氏度）

P: Sir, you've got a fever.

先生，您发烧了。

（其他乘务员配合腾置隔离区）

FA: We will arrange more space for you. You could lie down and have a good rest. Please stay calm and we will look after you well. We'll contact the ground authorities and look for medical professional volunteers On-board.

我们将为您腾置空座，您可以到后排躺下来以便得到良好的休息。别担心，我们会照顾好您。我们会联系地面，并帮您寻找医生。

P: OK. Thanks!

好的，谢谢！

FA: Are you traveling with any companions?

您有一起旅行的同伴吗？

P: No, just me.

没有，就我一个。

FA: This way, please.

请跟我来。

乘务员收集病患旅客信息

FA: Would you please tell me your full medical history, symptoms and recent travel history?

请告诉我您的病史、病症以及近期旅行史。

寻找医护人员机上广播

Ladies and gentlemen, may I have your attention, please? One of our passengers On-board needs immediate medical attention. If you are medical professional volunteers, please identify yourself to any cabin crew. Thank you!

女士们、先生们，现在飞机上有一位生病的旅客需要帮助。如果您是医生或护士，请立即与乘务员联系。谢谢！

乘务员安抚周边旅客并收集信息

FA: Excuse me, Madam. The passenger over there just now coughed a lot. We have taken the temperature, about 38.5℃. Here're masks and gloves for you for the sake of your health.

刚才那位旅客咳嗽的比较厉害，发烧38.5度。为了您的健康，我们为您提供了口罩和手套。

P: OK. Thanks！

好的，谢谢！

FA: Excuse me? Would you please fill in this form in case we contact you later?

请您填写一下个人信息，方便我们跟您取得联系。

飞机降落机上广播

Ladies and gentlemen, the Port Health Office will meet our aircraft. It is a standard procedure for authorities to request us to remain on the aircraft. Please remain in your seats until we are able to advise you further. Thank you for your patience and cooperation!

女士们、先生们，飞机到达地面后，按照规定的程序，将有卫生检疫部门的人员登机。请你保持就座，等待进一步的指示。感谢你的耐心和配合！

高频语句

01 We will stay with you and I will inform my manager.

我们会一直陪着您，同时我将报告我们乘务长。

02 Please carry on the universal precautions procedure and pay close attention to the passenger.

请立即做好个人防护，密切关注旅客。

03 Dear Sir, may I take your temperature, please?

先生，给您量一下体温。

相关表达　Sir, could I take the temperature, please?

04 We will arrange more space for you.

我们将为您腾置空座。

05 We'll contact the ground authorities and look for medical professional volunteers On-board.

我们会联系地面，并帮您寻找医生。

06 Would you please tell me your full medical history, symptoms and recent travel history?
请告诉我您的病史、病症以及近期旅行史。

07 If you are medical professional volunteers, please identify yourself to any cabin crew.
如果您是医生或护士，请立即与乘务员联系。

08 Here're masks and gloves for you for the sake of your health.
为了您的健康，我们为您提供了口罩和手套。
相关表达　For the sake of your health, please wear masks and gloves.

专业词汇

suspected infectious diseases　疑似传染病　　medical history　病史
symptoms　症状　　　　　　　　　　　　　　masks and gloves　口罩和手套

拓展知识

Travel by air during coronavirus outbreak

I. Is it safe to travel by air?

Airports and airlines are trying to minimize the risks of contagions in their often-crowded environments. The reality is that the air quality on an airplane is actually really good—high amounts of clean outdoor air and all recirculated air passes through a HEPA filter. The risk of transmission On-board is significantly reduced.

Some destinations require proof of a negative COVID-19 test; other destinations test passengers on arrival. Many have mandatory 14-day quarantines.

II. What protective measures could a passenger take On-board?

Better to wear a facemask to board planes. Bring alcohol-based antiseptic wipes with you. Avoid touching eyes, mouth and nose. If possible, keep social distance with other passengers and try to avoid close contact. Try to use the lavatory less.

III. What if encountering a suspected medical case?

In case of suspected infectious disease on board, the flight allendants will arrange more space for the passenger in a quarantine area in the back of the cabin. The lavatory on the right side of the rear cabin will be reserved for that passenger accordingly, so as to avoid cross infection.

疫情防控期间搭乘飞机

一、搭乘飞机安全吗？

航空公司竭力降低人员密集场所的感染风险。事实上，飞机在设计时已经考虑了运行过程中的通风要求，空气循环系统和过滤功能可大大降低病毒在飞机上扩散蔓延的可能性。

各地会根据不同等级的疫情防控要求，请旅客出示核酸检测结果，对旅客进行核酸检测，进行14天隔离管理等。

二、坐飞机如何做好个人防护？

佩戴口罩。随身携带一些含酒精类的消毒湿巾。乘机过程中尽量不用双手触摸眼睛、鼻子和嘴巴。有可能的条件下，旅客间保持一定距离，尽量避免直接接触。尽量减少使用卫生间。

三、如果客机上发现旅客有疑似传染病症状怎么办？

如果客机上发现了旅客有疑似传染病症状，工作人员会将旅客安置在机上相对隔离区，同时会把飞机右后侧的卫生间，留以专用，避免和其他旅客共用造成交叉感染。

案例分析

飞机客舱空气每2到3分钟置换一次，每小时置换20到30次。飞机通风系统主要使空气上下流动，这种循环方式可以有效降低病毒在飞机上扩散蔓延的可能。医院手术室的空气更换速率是12分钟更换一次，普通建筑的更换率则更低。

问题 飞机上，如果有疑似新冠、埃博拉等传染病症状旅客，乘务员应当如何处置？

参考答案

确认旅客有典型传染病症状后，立即报告乘务长、机长，周知乘务组，启动公共医疗卫生事件应急处置流程，机组人员互相配合共同完成处置任务。乘务员进行个人防护，由专职乘务员照看疑似传染病旅客，将其安排至隔离区，准备好氧气瓶，定时检测心跳和脉搏，询问疑似传染病旅客的个人信息、病史、旅居史、生病典型症状等，收集旅客污染物至黄色医疗垃圾袋中封存，喷洒消毒剂。其他机组人员配合寻找空座位，设置隔离区，进行客舱广播寻求医生帮助，做好周边旅客的情绪安抚，提供防护用品，收集周边旅客信息。乘务长填写《机上突发疾病记录表》、《机上紧急医学事件报告单》等表单。根据卫生检疫部门指示进行进一步处理。